What People Are Saying About
Everyday Faith for Daily Life

Jan writes with the warmth of a cozy fireplace, beckoning your heart and mind to join in her experiences. She draws from her vast history and present happenings. You feel settled and comfortable as you read her reflections. She knows how to bring a story to life.

Mark Rhoades, National Administrator
AG Marriage Encounter

I want to commend Jan White for a clever, but practically written book on everyday life...*Everyday Faith*. Most of us look for God during the benchmark moments of our life, but He is with us...and teaches us every day. The real genius is not someone who can take a simple problem and make it complex, but the one who can take the complex and make it simple. Jan White has accomplished this in her new book. You will want to read this book, and then read it again!

Scott Dawson, Founder and CEO
Scott Dawson Evangelistic Association

Knowing Jan and enjoying her friendship has been a blessing. She always has a smile, a friendly word, and an encouraging spirit for all those who cross her path. Much thought and prayer has gone into every word that's being shared in this book. Words can tear down or build up...she is a builder.

Brenda Gantt, Social Media Influencer
"Cooking with Brenda Gantt"

Everyday Faith
for
Daily Life

Everyday Faith
for
Daily Life

Jan White

DEDICATION

This book is dedicated to my parents, grandparents, and my husband's parents whose legacy of faith has shown me how to live my faith. I am grateful for this Godly heritage.

CONTENTS

FOREWORD

Faith in and of itself is not a struggle. However, for us to consistently grow in our faith, sinful as we are … well that is a daily struggle … at least for me. Occasionally though, I encounter someone who is seemingly always on the advance, and their advancement in the faith is a true and genuine encouragement to me. My friend, Jan White, is one of the few who exemplifies Christ in all that she is … especially in her writings. Through the years, Jan has lifted me during trying times, either through her calming presence or her reassuring prose. Most of the time she never realized the effectiveness of her presence. To know her, truly is to love her … and for those of us fortunate enough to know her, we are blessed.

Even if you do not know Jan, you soon will. In the pages that follow, Jan has poured out the ink of the Holy Spirit onto the parchment that is the body of Christ. No doubt, you will find her words as comforting and Spirit-filled as I did. And, Jan does not write for her own glory. In fact, throughout her life, Jan has written almost exclusively for the cause of Christ. Oft-times declining a by-line, Jan's desire is to spread the comfort that Christ brings. But Jan's writing is unique: separated from the prose of most Christian writers, her down-to-earth approach does not only deliver an evangelical message, it also offers real world anecdotes peppered with the Gospel's significance. No, friend, this book is not "just another Christian book." *Everyday Faith for Daily Life* is a unique merger of entertaining true-life accounts, either from biblical times or the more modern era, coupled with the life lessons that the Bible has to offer to its reader.

This book is also a reflection of Jan. It is subtle and poignant. Her stories slip in unnoticed, only to captivate you with the Biblical moral and leave you profoundly impacted by their truths. I was at times overcome with awe of God's presence; other times I was overcome with appreciation for God's grace; and yes…, at times, tears flowed. Her stories and lessons challenged me. They inspired me. They lifted me up and drew me nearer. These are not only her words, but also the epitome of Jan's spirit. Much like the chorus of one of her favorite hymns, Jan can truly proclaim, "This is my story, this is my song, praising my Savior all the day long."

Life is hard. I can certainly attest to that. As the District Attorney for the 22nd Judicial Circuit of the State of Alabama, I see the wages of sin manifested daily. Addiction, thievery, immorality, hatred, anger, and so much more, fill the coffers of the court system with a deposit of human decline that is rarely counteracted by the work of men. Lawyers and judges, try as they might, well-intended though they may be, look for redemption for the accused in subjective surveys and studies of the human condition. What most overlook is the one thing Jan so easily identifies in the passages that follow … hope and redemption are only found in Christ Jesus.

Christians often miss the practical application of the Gospel when witnessing to others. That is…, how the Gospel will affect their earthly life. Careful though we are not to promote a false prosperity Gospel, the reality is that acceptance of the Gospel brings change, and that change in someone's life can bring about profoundly positive consequences. Many drug addicts who tried every other man-made remedy and failed, find sobriety through the power of the Gospel. Lonely middle-aged men, depressed and questioning whether they have the wherewithal to face another day, find the sufficiency of companionship with Jesus because of the Gospel. Marriages on the brink of destruction find restoration because one party, or the other, or both, accept the truth of the Gospel and submit to Christ. The power of the Gospel has very real consequences here on earth, and I thank God for it.

Matthew 11:28 (KJV) recorded Jesus' invitation to the weak and the weary ... "Come to me all ye that labour and are heavy laden and I will give you rest." *Everyday Faith for Daily Life* is so often a demonstration of what happens when we surrender in our weakness to Jesus, and He gives us rest. I do not know what troubles you, the reader, as you shuffle through these first few pages. I do not even know why you bought the book..., but something drew you to it. Do not stop now. There is power and authority in these pages that I know will bring you rest.

A few years ago, I stood at the top of an arena where a couple of thousand men had come together for study and worship. A small group of men, myself included, organized the event with the hope of spurring revival in men. I was exhausted, and honestly ... a little reluctant. I surveyed the crowd and watched Scott Dawson, an old friend of Jan's and mine, take the stage. I truly was in awe that God used us to assemble a group of men this large in one place to "worship His Holy Name." Scott shared with me before he took the stage that he needed prayer. "I am going to start this conference with the Gospel message," he said. "2,000 Christian men, and the Lord keeps telling me to tell them who His Son is and give them an invitation." I was reluctant for the very reason he already knew ... these were the backbone of the church, not your Easter and Christmas crowd, but the 'every time the doors are open' crowd. And 'this is the beginning of a two-day conference' … 'you should do the invitation at the end,' I thought to myself.

My reluctance was doubtless mixed with pride. I doubted God's timing, and my pride told me I knew better than He did.

Scott delivered a powerful Gospel message and opened the arena floor for men to come forward and profess their repentance and confession and new commitment to Christ. I bowed my head and began to pray. I prayed in earnest that God would move these mountains we call men. Tears began to flow down my cheeks … they do now also, for it is still such a powerful memory … tears flowed because, as I prayed, I became keenly aware of my own doubt and pride.

I turned the attention of my prayer inward, and I asked God to move the mountain of pride within me … and He did. It was a powerful few minutes of prayer, and I knew God brought Scott and his message to remind me to trust in Him. I smiled as I opened my eyes, feeling sort of like Jonah, and chuckled as I realized how much God had taught me in the last few minutes. I wiped the tears from my eyes, and looked up … Over 200 men were kneeling at the altar. Scott, overwhelmed by how much Jesus had just shown up, was calling for pastors to come from the audience to help disciple and pray with these men. I melted … in awe of knowing that I truly was sitting in the presence of God.

We brought a few loaves of bread and a couple of fish that day. God showed up and fed the entire crowd … and along the way, he brought 234 men into the sheepfold protection of the His grace. And to think, I doubted He could do it. I love it when God reminds me that He is greater.

What does a men's conference at that arena have to do with Jan White? Well … those men who came to that arena are probably not unlike you or me. Everyone who left that arena knew they had witnessed something amazing. Everyone experienced God. You will experience God in this book as well. One of the practical dangers of life is becoming more faithful to our 'routine' of everyday faith than we are faithful to Jesus. That is when we know God but do not experience Him. That is when we need to be shaken. At least 234 men walked into that rural country arena comfortable in the everyday routine of faith ... many of them, only knowing God. They left shaken by Him, and now they walk joyfully in the stronghold of a relationship of everyday faith in Jesus.

As you peruse the pages of this *Everyday Faith*, I pray it shakes you. I pray it draws you nearer to Christ.

Fight the good fight, keep the faith, finish the race.

Walt Merrell, District Attorney
22nd Judicial Circuit, State of Alabama

INTRODUCTION

My love of words began in third grade when our teacher read a chapter of *Charlotte's Web* by E.B. White every day after lunch. I couldn't wait to find out what happened to Wilbur and all the other characters in the barnyard. My imagination was captured by the power of the story.

My love of words sparked an interest in taking writing courses in college. I graduated with a B.S. degree with majors in History and English/Journalism. My love of words competes with my love of history. After a couple of years as a writer for a ministry, our family moved to my husband's hometown in south Alabama.

I worked for a weekly newspaper and then a bi-weekly newspaper in the county. While I was a young mother, I wrote free-lance articles for magazines, devotional guides, and other publications. Our family owned a Christian bookstore for a number of years, so I was surrounded by books of all genres and I learned about publishing from the retailer side.

Then, one day, the publisher of our local newspaper came into the bookstore and asked if I would like to write a religion column. He knew about my previous newspaper work. I agreed, and over 25 years later, I continue to write a weekly column for the *Andalusia Star-News*, missing only the week when Hurricane Opal knocked out our electricity, and once while I was recovering from surgery. The *Enterprise Southeast Sun* began publishing my column over 15 years ago. Based on the circulation numbers of these newspapers, I have the privilege of speaking through the printed page to thousands of people, a privilege I take seriously and prayerfully.

My newspaper experience prepared me to write columns that will hook the readers in the first sentence so they will give me a few minutes of their time to read my message. My goal has always been to give them a "take-away" by the last sentence – a point to ponder that may speak to them another day.

One of the *Andalusia Star-News* editors gave my column the name – *Everyday Faith* – thus the title for this book. *Everyday Faith for Daily Life* is a compilation of some of my most memorable columns. In this book, I share personal experiences, inspirational stories, and practical lessons from my life that have inspired my faith. I enjoy writing on a variety of topics.

Every week I pray, "Lord, what do You want me to write in this week's column?" My prayer becomes more urgent the closer I get to the deadline. Many years ago, while journaling one day, God spoke to my heart the words that every Christian writer needs to remember, "Your words don't change hearts. I change hearts with your words."

Having a weekly deadline requires discipline. I call it "writing aerobics." Coming up with an idea every week can be challenging. A blank computer screen can be intimidating. I figure if a topic is interesting to me it could be interesting to my readers. There are certain seasons of life that most of us have in common. These experiences lend themselves to good column material, because most of us have experienced or will experience them. For instance, I once wrote a column when our daughter was learning to drive, and I was struggling with getting out of the driver's seat. There are times throughout life when we must let go…whatever the situation.

My love of history gives me ideas for my weekly religion column. I've written about lessons learned from the sinking of the Titanic, the life of St. Patrick, and the history behind our most beloved hymns. Sometimes an idea comes from an event like the 400th Anniversary of the Book that Changed the World (the King James Version of the Bible) and little-known facts about man walking on the moon…or as Paul Harvey used to say – "the rest of the story."

From time to time during the past 25 years, readers have commented about how a particular column spoke to them. Some folks have told me they have a folder of my columns clipped from the newspaper, that they share with family members or their Sunday School class. Hearing their positive feedback gives me encouragement to keep on keeping on. There have been a few people who took the time to let me know they did not agree with a topic. I learn from those comments too, because they give me a perspective I may not have considered. Negative comments show me the variety of people who read my words.

I believe God ordains that certain people cross our paths during our lifetime. When our family moved to south Alabama, I was introduced to Lou Brown and her husband, Pat. The story of their courtship reminds me of one of my favorite novels, *Christy*, written by Catherine Marshall. Miz Lou, as people knew her, also wrote a regular column in the *Andalusia Star-News*. She began writing her column in the 1950's, continuing until the 1970's.

Her descriptive, homespun writing taught me how words can paint a picture about daily life. Readers could see the glory of God's creation by reading her column – *My Country Roads*. When she was diagnosed with cancer, I felt it urgent to ask her if I could write her biography. She replied, "What if we get started and I kick the bucket?" She did not think her life story worthy of a biography. One of my hobbies is collecting her old columns so they do not fade like newsprint from the memories of people who never got to read her words. At times, I feel like I am following in her footsteps.

In 1994, I met one of the godliest and most humble men I've ever known. A quiet, unassuming businessman named Jim Russell spoke at the Florida Christian Writers Conference. He's another person I believe God planned to cross my path during my lifetime. He came to encourage

Christians to write for the secular market, especially newspapers. I attended his workshop. At that time, he said surveys found that most readers turn to the editorial page first, giving Christian writers a great opportunity to speak to thousands of people about scriptural principles, even if only through writing letters to the editor.

Mr. Russell emphasized the power of the printed Word of God, based on the promise in Isaiah 55:11 (NKJV), "It shall not return unto me void. But it shall accomplish what I please, and it shall prosper in the thing for which I sent it." He stressed writing the truth in love, concisely and accurately, and including a verse of Scripture. Whether or not a reader understands or agrees with my words, God's Word will accomplish what He intends.

Jim Russell, using his own money, established the Amy Foundation, named for his daughter with developmental disabilities. The Amy Foundation sponsored the Amy Writing Award to encourage Christian writers to submit to secular media. I submitted columns for the Amy Writing Award for ten years and never even placed, not even honorable mention. When the 11th competition came around, I wondered whether I should submit anything. I decided to submit once more, and that year I won the top prize – the Amy Writing Award.

God also planned for me to meet Chuck Colson, whose year-long Christian Worldview study taught me how to love the Lord with my mind and to live out "a biblical view of all of life" in today's culture. The Centurion Program, now called the Colson Fellows Program, included three weekends with Chuck Colson and other speakers who are the best and brightest in apologetics (the defense of the divine origin and the authority of Christianity).

Chuck Colson founded the program "to equip serious Christians to think seriously about all of life's issues; to become change agents to strengthen the church and in turn the culture for generations to come." I am still digesting the

Truth I learned during that year and I go back to the assigned books and to my notes. It's not enough to know what you believe. You must know why you believe it.

I feel as though I am standing on the shoulders of these people, and many others, who inspired and influenced my faith and my writing career. Growing up in a family with multi-generations of ministers gave me deep insights into God's Word and how to apply it to daily life. Through the years, I've attended Christian Writers Conferences and learned from other authors and publishers about how to polish my writing.

Holocaust survivor Corrie ten Boom once wrote, "Books do not age as you and I do. They will speak still when we are gone, to generations we will never see. Yes, the books must survive." That's one reason for compiling a selection of eighty columns that I felt worthy of being included in a book. Through the years, readers have encouraged me to publish my columns in a book. It's been a labor of love to search my archives of columns to choose the words you will read.

Job 19:23 (KJV) is one of my favorite verses in the Bible, "Oh that my words were now written! oh, that they were printed in a book!" I've been privileged to help other people write their books. Now, I hold the fulfillment of my heart's desire of many years. I once heard someone say, "The faintest ink is better than the strongest memory." This book preserves messages in my column that I trust will continue to speak to people in years to come.

I believe your faith will be inspired as you read this book. I hope you will experience some "aha" moments that enlighten your perspective on a particular topic. My prayer is you will come away with a stronger faith for your daily life!

Jan White

LIFE IS ALWAYS
THE MOST BEAUTIFUL CHOICE

Though the missionary couple had four children, they began asking God for another child. They even prayed for "Timmy" by name.

Bob and Pam and their family had moved to the Philippines in 1985 to take the Gospel to those who have never heard and plant Bible-believing churches where there were no churches. Just before she became pregnant, Pam contracted amoebic dysentery, transmitted through contaminated drinking water, and fell into a coma.

According to a news article about the family, Pam's treatment required a series of strong medications. Even though she discontinued the medications when she found out she was pregnant, doctors strongly advised her to have an abortion. They thought the fetus had been irreversibly damaged as a result of the medications and expected the baby to be stillborn.

Pam would not consider aborting because of her faith in God. In the seventh month of her pregnancy, she traveled to the country's capital, Manila, to receive around-the-clock care. She had to spend the last two months of her pregnancy on bed rest. Pam continued to pray for a healthy child.

On her due date – August 24, 1987 – she gave birth to a healthy baby boy, whom she described as "skinny, but rather long."

Three years later, Bob and Pam and their family moved back to the U.S. But they continued to return to the Philippines every year as volunteers to work in an orphanage and other ministry outreaches there.

Their youngest son, who his mother calls "Timmy," is

over thirty years old, stands 6'3" tall and weighs 235 pounds. He excelled in football and became a highly recruited quarterback. His high school stats include 95 passing touchdowns and 62 rushing touchdowns.

He chose to attend the University of Florida, not so much because his parents were graduates of the school, but because he felt best suited for their "spread option" offense. As a true freshman, he helped the Gators win the national championship in college football. Coach Urban Meyer has described him as the "sparkplug" of the Gator offense.

On December 8, 2007, Tim Tebow won the Heisman trophy, the first college sophomore to win in the 70-plus years of the award. He's been called an All-American and athletic hero.

Bob Tebow has said his son is "a miracle baby" and they've reminded him of that hundreds of times. The Tebows had no way of knowing God's plan for their unborn son, but they did realize that every life is precious.

The Bible says that God knows us before we are born (Jeremiah 1:5). "For You formed my inward parts; You covered me in my mother's womb. I will praise You, for I am fearfully and wonderfully made; Your eyes saw my substance, being yet unformed," (Psalm 139:13, 14 & 16 NKJ).

Life is always the most beautiful choice.

FORGIVENESS BREAKS
THE CHAINS OF HATRED

A horrible tragedy occurred in rural Pennsylvania in October 2006 when a gunman walked into a one-room Amish schoolhouse and killed five schoolgirls.

It's inconceivable the evil that one person is capable of committing against innocent human lives. The Amish community - grieving their great loss - asked for prayer and privacy, following the shooting rampage that also wounded five other girls.

News reports of the shocking tragedy tell of a disturbed man filled with hate toward himself, hate toward God, and "unimaginable emptiness." In the aftermath of the tragic event, reporters have repeatedly been amazed that the Amish people have emphasized the need for forgiveness, not anger, toward the gunman.

"We're very concerned that no message of revenge gets out. We believe in forgiveness," an Amish man was quoted as saying. Another said, "We want to forgive. That's the way we were brought up – turn good for evil."

It's inconceivable that a community suffering such a senseless tragedy could make contact with the gunman's family with the message of forgiveness. Amish elders went to meet with the gunman's widow. Marie Roberts was reportedly invited to attend the girls' funerals.

One Amish woman said, "We can tell people about Christ, and actually show you in our walk that we can forgive; not just say it, but in our walk of life. You know you have to live it; you can't just say it."

Watching and reading about these Amish people, I thought of the saying, "Preach the Gospel, and if necessary, use words." They preached to the world the forgiveness of Christ who, while dying on a cross said, "Father, forgive them, for they do not know what they do" (Luke 23:34 NKJ).

One newsman made reference to the statement, "To err is human, to forgive divine." Extending forgiveness in this situation would be humanly impossible were it not for their faith in Christ that enables them to show His compassion.

What is forgiveness? "Forgiveness is surrendering my right to hurt you for hurting me," according to psychologist Archibald Hart. "Everyone says forgiveness is a lovely idea, until they have something to forgive," C.S. Lewis once said.

Hopefully, you and I will never have to forgive someone for something so horrendous as murdering our children. But, are we willing to forgive the friend or family member who hurt us this week or even many years ago? Sometimes we find it hard to forgive ourselves.

Holocaust survivor Corrie Ten Boom has written, "Forgiveness is the key that unlocks the door of resentment and the handcuffs of hate. It is a power that breaks the chains of bitterness and the shackles of selfishness."

Ann Curry, a Today Show anchor, commented after covering the tragic event, "I realize I did not know what forgiveness was until now." Would someone learn the meaning of forgiveness by looking at our lives?

LETTING GO MEANS
ABANDONING THE DRIVER'S SEAT

It took me by surprise. Maybe it was because I hadn't expected this day to come so soon. Then again, I don't remember giving any thought to what this day would be like anyway.

I could feel the tension tightening inside of me. The knots in my stomach were the size of the white knuckles on my hands.

Though empty-handed, I was holding on for dear life, watching time slip through my fingers. There I sat looking at the child I'd held in my arms 15 years ago. The same little girl whose hand I used to grasp to cross the street.

"It's so hard to believe," I kept telling myself. But a wallet-size, plastic card with her picture on it made it official.

Before my very eyes, my daughter was sitting in the driver's seat behind the steering wheel of our car. It was difficult for me to accept the fact that my daughter had a permit to learn to drive.

This brought another frightening realization. Considering how many ninth graders there are in the city and county, imagine how many teenagers are learning to drive on the streets and roads we travel every day.

"Everybody who's ever driven a vehicle had to learn how to drive," my husband, Greg, reminded me. His words couldn't console this mother's nervousness. Thankfully, he volunteered to be the driving instructor of the family.

As for me, I gave new meaning to the term "backseat driver." I couldn't resist asking if she was going too fast or staying in the center of her lane, etc., etc. My eyes were alert at every intersection. Oncoming traffic was alarming as our car would meet another vehicle in the opposite lane.

"Lord, keep the other driver on their side of the road." I not only prayed that for my daughter, but for everyone else on the highway. Letting my child learn to drive has also given new meaning to prayer.

From other mothers, I've been told I will be praying even more when she's old enough to drive without a parent. I don't want to even think about that day.

Now I know why it's required for a teenager to have a permit for one year before getting their license. It takes a year for mothers like me to get used to the idea.

With practice, Kelley's driving has improved. She's getting more confident; but, more importantly, I'm more confident about it. Even though, the "letting go" hasn't been easy for me.

Have you ever had a hard time letting go? I've found it usually means I must get out of the "driver's seat." In other words, I must admit I can't handle a situation or problem. It's a lesson we all have to learn at some time or another. And it often requires prayer.

"Lord, it's so hard to believe this is happening to me. No matter how difficult, help me accept the fact You are the only One who can steer me through this time."

IT'S A WONDERFUL LIFE ...
EVERY LIFE IS SPECIAL

Who can forget Jimmy Stewart's portrayal of George Bailey in the movie classic, *"It's a Wonderful Life?"*

Every time I watch it, I get a lump in my throat at the end of the movie when George comes running into his house and joyfully embraces his wife and children. He's a changed man who has come back from the depths of despair.

Financial problems caused George to consider jumping from a snow-covered bridge into the river to end his life. But God sends an angel named Clarence to rescue him.

"I wish I'd never been born," George tells his guardian angel. Clarence looks heavenward and their supernatural journey begins. George Bailey finds out how everyone else's life would have been different if he'd never lived.

His younger brother, Harry, drowns at age nine because George isn't there to rescue him when he falls through thin ice while skating on a pond. As a result, Harry would have never grown up to be a war hero whose act of bravery saved all the lives of the men on a Navy transport during the war.

Mr. Gower, the druggist, would have given poisonous pills to a family with diphtheria, but George recognized the grieving man's mistake and prevented the tragedy.

George Bailey is horrified to see that without the impact of his life, everything about his community was sadly different...from the name of the town, to its businesses and, especially his friends and neighbors. He joyfully returns to reality, realizing he truly has a wonderful life.

This movie classic gives us a vivid picture of the value of every human life; not just George's, but his wife and children and people in his town. As Clarence says, "Every man's life touches so many other lives, and when he isn't around, he leaves an awful hole."

"*It's a Wonderful Life*" shows how every one of us has a role in life that only we can play. The value of human life comes from knowing that God has a purpose for each of our lives that we are born to fulfill. By the end of the movie, George learns "no man is a failure who has friends."

The Bible says God knew us before we were born (Jeremiah 1:5). He made us in His image (Genesis 1:27). I believe human life has lost some of its value in the eyes of many over the past 47 years. Since 1973, when the U.S. Supreme Court made abortion on demand legal during the entire nine months of pregnancy, over 60 million lives have been ended before they were born.

We will never know the impact their lives would have had on the world around them. Could one of them have been the scientist with the intellect to find the cure for cancer or AIDS? A future president? An astronaut? A pro-athlete? Or a George Bailey?

God "gives to all life, breath, and all things" (Acts 17:25 NKJ). Only He knows when life should begin and end.

KNOWING HYMN'S HISTORY
MAKES SINGING IT MORE MEANINGFUL

Hymns are woven into the fabric of our lives. Singing one of my favorite hymns can take me back to my childhood and my memories of growing up in church. Hymns transcend time because their messages speak to everyday needs like suffering, tragedy, and living the Christian life.

"A good hymn should be like a good prayer - simple, real, earnest, and reverent," one hymn writer has said. Hymns inspire hope, trust, and faith by reminding us of God's love and care each day, and of eternal life in heaven. Many hymns were penned in the face of adversity and sorrow.

Eugene Bartlett, a noted music teacher, wrote several hundred hymns, often in a matter of minutes. Then, near the end of his life he suffered a stroke that left him confined to his bed, unable to speak. Bartlett demonstrated his faith in spite of his condition and spent almost one month writing the words and music to *Victory in Jesus*.

One of the most prolific hymn writers of all time was Fanny Crosby, estimated to have written 8,000 to 9,000 hymn texts. Open the pages of any hymnal and you'll find her songs such as *"Pass Me Not, O Gentle Savior,"* and *"Have Thine Own Way, Lord."* My favorite Crosby hymn is *"Blessed Assurance."* I especially like the words of the chorus, "This is my story, this is my song, praising my Savior all the day long."

Fanny Crosby was known for her poetry before she began writing Gospel songs. What makes her remarkable is that she was blind from six weeks of age due to improper medical treatment. During her 95 years of life, she memorized entire books of the Bible.

Horatio Spafford invested in real estate in Chicago, along the shores of Lake Michigan. Much of it burned up in the Chicago Fire of 1871. His family decided to take a trip for much-needed rest and to help with an evangelistic campaign in Great Britain. Due to last minute business issues, he sent his wife and four daughters ahead, expecting to follow them aboard another ship a few days later.

The ship on which his family sailed struck another ship and sank. His wife cabled her husband from Wales that she alone survived. As he sailed across the ocean to join his wife, he was told about the approximate location of the ship on which his children perished. Then he began writing, "When peace like a river attendeth my way, when sorrows like sea billows roll, whatever my lot, Thou hast taught me to say, It is well, it is well with my soul."

Knowing these hymn histories make the songs even more meaningful to sing. The Bible instructs us to speak to "one another in psalms and hymns and spiritual songs, singing and making melody in your heart to the Lord" (Ephesians 5:19 NKJ).

A great theologian once held up a Bible before a sermon and said, "This is the Gospel." And then in the other hand, he held up a hymnal and continued, "And this is how we remember it."

WINNING AND LOSING DEPENDS ON WHETHER YOU'RE "SAFE AT HOME"

"Every day is a new opportunity. You can build on yesterday's success," pitcher Bob Feller once said, "Or put its failures behind and start over again." He went on to say that's the way it is in baseball and that's the way it is in life.

This popular sport that we call the "national pastime" impacts the way we talk. If an action requires special courage, we challenge someone to "step up to the plate." Then again, if he or she wants to attempt something we think will fail, we discourage them by saying, "You won't get to first base."

If a person is doing everything right, we tell them they're "batting a thousand." When someone's tremendously successful, they have "knocked a homerun." When we consider someone else's thinking more extreme than ours, we say the person with an opposing view is "out in left field." I cannot "cover all the bases" without some interesting parallels from the Bible.

What does the Bible have to say about baseball? Take another look at Genesis 1:1. "In the 'big-inning' God created the heaven and the earth." All kidding aside, I believe, "In the beginning God created the heaven and the earth."

In baseball, a sacrifice occurs when a batter bunts or hits a ball and makes an out, allowing a base runner to advance. The Bible says Jesus came "to put away sin by the sacrifice of Himself" (Hebrews 9:26 NKJ). Jesus gave His life for us, allowing us to be on His team.

In the game of baseball, there's a five-sided plate where you plant your feet and swing a bat before going to first base. It's also the place where you must return after running to all the bases to score. Winning or losing depends on it.

Home represents two Biblical principles. First, it's a place we can come back to. Remember the prodigal son who demanded his father give him his inheritance? The boy went to a far country, wasted his money on wild living, ending up in a pig pen. When he returned home, his father was waiting with open arms to welcome his son and celebrated his homecoming.

I recently learned that shortly before his death in 1961, baseball Hall-of-Famer Ty Cobb came to faith in Christ. Biographers tell how Cobb, who grew up in rural north Georgia, was known for his outbursts of anger and drinking made it worse. He said, "Tell the boys that I'm sorry I waited until the bottom of the ninth to get right with God. I wish now that I had done it in the top of the first."

Home can also represent heaven. There's a grandstand there where loved ones who have gone on before us are cheering us on (Hebrews 12:1). Accept Jesus' sacrifice for your sins. You can be "safe at Home" in heaven eternally. Your Heavenly Father is waiting with open arms for you to come home. "Three strikes and you're out" is the rule in baseball and criminal records, but not with God. "If we confess our sins, He is faithful and just to forgive us our sins and to cleanse us from all unrighteousness" (1 John 1:9 NKJ).

MUCH OF OUR EVERYDAY LANGUAGE COMES FROM THE BIBLE

I am a collector. I guess that explains why a pack rat like me saves so much stuff. One day it occurred to me that if a mouse squeaks, a pack rat would squeal, "Keep it, keep it, keep it!"

My collections include postage stamps, old books and Bibles, presidential campaign memorabilia, anything by or about C.S. Lewis, and last, but not least, family history. I also collect quotes and old sayings and research on their origin. Did you know many old sayings spoken every day come from the Bible?

If someone says you're as "old as Methuselah," you are beyond retirement age. He lived to be 969 years old, the oldest man listed in the Bible. If you help someone in need, someone may call you a "Good Samaritan."

When asked how a mutual friend or family member is doing, folks sometimes reply, "Am I my brother's keeper?" That was Cain's answer in Genesis 4:9 when God confronted him about killing his brother.

Still today, when someone behaves badly that person is "raising Cain." The parenting principle, "spare the rod, spoil the child" is based on Proverbs 13:24. If a child says something remarkable for his or her age, you might hear the comment "out of the mouth of babes."

"To kill the fatted calf" refers to preparations for a joyful occasion because that is what the father of the prodigal son did in Luke 15:11-32. "To turn the other cheek" and not strike someone in return for injury or insult comes from Jesus' teaching in Luke 6:29. Jesus also talked about the "blind leading the blind" in Luke 6:39.

Have you ever said that you "wash your hands" of a situation? It means to refuse to accept responsibility for something and it comes from Matthew 27:24 when Pontius Pilate washed his hands before allowing Jesus to be put to death.

If you see the "handwriting on the wall" warning of danger, you may also find "your days are numbered." The prophet Daniel interpreted a message written by a mysterious hand that informed King Belshazzar his kingdom was about to be overthrown. Read Daniel chapter six.

Unexpected assistance is often referred to as "manna from heaven," as in the food that miraculously appeared to feed the Israelites on their journey from Egypt to the Promised Land. See Exodus 16:15. If you are made the scapegoat, you get all the blame. Read about the reason for a scapegoat on the Day of Atonement in Leviticus 16.

Some sayings like "jumping Jehoshaphat" or "land o' Goshen" are exclamations of surprise using the name of an Old Testament king of Judah and the fertile land in Egypt where the Israelites lived.

This collection of words and phrases proves once again that the Bible is a timeless book. One can spend a lifetime learning the truth on its pages. "Lord willing," I'll keep studying this best-selling book of all time and find more old sayings to live by.

FUNNY STORY
TEACHES LESSON ON PRIDE

Have you ever heard the story about the frog from Minnesota who wanted to escape the cold temperatures? He decided to find a way to go south for the winter.

Two geese nearby were about to start their flight southward for their annual migration. The frog asked them, "Will you take me with you?" At first, they refused. They didn't see how it could be done. But the frog devised a plan.

He convinced each of them to hold either end of a short stick in their beaks. Then, he said he would hold on in the middle with his mouth. The unlikely threesome took off, and sure enough the frog's plan worked.

During their flight southward, as they traveled over Indiana, a farmer looked up into the clear, blue skies. He remarked loudly, "What a clever idea! I wonder which one of them came up with that remarkable idea!" The frog could be heard yelling, "I diiiiddd!" as he plummeted to earth.

"Pride goes before destruction and a haughty spirit before a fall," according to the wise words of Solomon in Proverbs 16:18 (NKJ). He lists the seven things the Lord hates and the first one is a proud look – seeing yourself as better than others. A New Testament writer declares, "God resists the proud, but gives grace to the humble" (James 4:6 NKJ).

British author G.K. Chesterton has remarked, "If I had only one sermon to preach, it would be a sermon against pride." Another Bible scholar believes pride is the ground from which all other sins grow.

Several years ago, a Christian music group, NewSong, recorded a song with catchy lyrics, "I, me, my, mine, pride will get you every time. Four words that spell decline, I, me, my, mine." I think it's interesting that the letter – i – is in the center of the word pride, since self-importance is a symptom of pride.

Benjamin Franklin wrote in his autobiography, "There is perhaps no one of our natural passions so hard to subdue as pride. Beat it down, stifle it, mortify it as much as one pleases, it is still alive. Even if I could conceive that I had completely overcome it, I should probably be proud of my humility."

Pride says, "My will be done." Humility says, "God's will be done." Christ Jesus, being one with God, made Himself of no reputation, took on the form of a servant, and came to earth as a man. In the Garden of Gethsemane, He prayed, "Nevertheless, not My will, but Yours be done" (Luke 22:42 NKJ). Then, He humbled Himself even further and died on the cross.

C.S. Lewis wrote, "As long as you are proud you cannot know God. A proud man is always looking down on things and people: and, of course, as long as you are looking down you cannot see something that is above you."

Someone once said that our Creator God may have been teaching us a lesson on pride when He made our human bodies. He designed us so it would be difficult to pat ourselves on the back.

GOD USES CRACKED POTS, IN SPITE OF THEIR FLAWS

A parable can teach a life lesson through a memorable story. I once heard a parable about a water bearer in China. The woman carried a long pole with two large water pots hanging on either end of the pole.

One of the pots was perfect and the other was cracked. The perfect pot always stayed full, except occasionally sloshing over the brim as the woman walked the long, dirt road from the stream to her house. But, by the time she sat the pair of pots down, half the liquid had leaked from the cracked pot.

This routine occurred every day for two years. The perfect pot proudly performed the task for which it was made. The cracked pot, ashamed of its imperfection, felt like a failure for accomplishing half of what it was made to do.

One day at the stream, the cracked pot spoke to the water bearer, "Because of my flaw, water leaks out all the way back to your house." The woman replied, "Did you notice that there are flowers only on your side of the path, but not on the other pot's side? That's because I have always known about your flaw, so I planted seeds on your side of the path.

"Every day while we walk back, you have watered them. For two years I have been able to pick these beautiful flowers to decorate my table. Without you being just the way you are, there would not be a bouquet to adorn the house."

What's the lesson of this parable? We are all cracked pots, with our own unique flaws. But, in spite of our shortcomings and failures, God can still use our lives according to His plans.

The story reminds me of the words of Isaiah who wrote, "But now, O Lord, you are our Father. We are the clay, you are the potter; we are all the work of your hand" (Isaiah 64:8 NKJ). Just like a potter shapes the clay into a pot, God can shape our lives into vessels useful for His work.

When Jesus walked the earth, He chose common people like fishermen to be His disciples, not the religious elite. The Apostle Paul once wrote, "Not many of you were wise by human standards; not many were influential; not many were of noble birth. But God chose the foolish things of the world to shame the wise; God chose the weak things of the world to shame the strong" (1 Corinthians 1:26-27 NIV).

Through the years, I've met people who know firsthand the love and forgiveness of Christ that delivers them from a life of addiction. It's amazing to see how God uses their lives to reach out and minister to others needing deliverance from the same sin. Many of us struggle with anxiety, fear, and other flaws too many to list.

Missionary Hudson Taylor has said, "All of God's giants have been weak men who did great things for God because they reckoned on his being with them." According to the Apostle Paul, God's grace is sufficient for us because His strength works best in our weakness.

WILL YOU LEND A HELPING HAND IN JESUS' NAME?

Holocaust survivor Corrie Ten Boom once wrote about her trip to Soviet Russia many years ago to visit an elderly lady who was a Christian.

Corrie and a friend climbed the steep steps to her one-room apartment at night to escape detection by the secret police. At that time, anyone caught even speaking the name of Jesus faced a death sentence.

As they entered the back door, the old woman's husband welcomed them. His frail wife was lying on a sofa, propped up on pillows, her body bent and twisted by multiple sclerosis.

Despite what the ravages of MS had done to her body, she had one finger she could control spasmodically. The woman's husband, who lovingly cared for her each day, placed an old typewriter in front of her on a table.

Peck...peck...pecking with that one finger, she translated portions of the Bible, as well as books by Billy Graham, Corrie Ten Boom, and Watchman Nee into Russian and Latvian. Corrie had come to thank her.

Looking at the woman with her head pulled down and feet curled back under her body, Corrie writes that she cried inwardly, asking why God didn't heal her? The old man sensed her anguish and answered, "God has a purpose in her sickness. Every other Christian in the city is watched by the secret police." He went on to say his wife had been sick for so long, they were left alone. She could type undetected.

This story gives us an inspiring example to follow. There's something, however small, that each of us can do to lend a helping hand to someone else. Yet so many times many of us do not lift a finger to serve in our churches or volunteer for charitable organizations like Meredith's Miracles, the Red Cross and Sav-A-Life.

Jesus said even giving a cup of cold water to a little one would be rewarded (Matthew 10:42). From His Words we get our Golden Rule, "Whatever you want men to do to you, do also to them" (Matthew 7:12 NKJ).

Earlier this week, I noticed a portion of a scripture on the side of the Arkansas Baptist Disaster Relief's vehicle, "For I was hungry and you gave Me food; I was thirsty and you gave Me drink." Matthew 25:35-36 goes on to say, "I was a stranger and you took Me in; I was naked and you clothed Me; I was sick and you visited Me; I was in prison and you came to Me" (NKJ).

Lending a helping hand takes time and money. Most of us have one of them, if not both. A few might only be able to pray for others. That's important too.

As one former president said, "Here on earth God's work must truly be our own." Will you lend a helping hand in Jesus' name?

ARE YOU WORTH YOUR SALT?

"The only thing necessary for evil to triumph is for good men to do nothing." These words were spoken by statesman Edmund Burke who served in the British Parliament over 200 years ago.

His words come to mind sometimes when I hear another shocking crime story on the ten o'clock news. It makes me question how anyone in our society could be capable of such evil.

An article I once read that was written by Dr. Dennis Kinlaw, president of the Francis Asbury Society, supplies some answers. He began by telling about his childhood during the Depression days.

Although he looked forward to the smell of bacon frying, he disliked the task of rubbing salt on pieces of pork to preserve the meat. One day, his mother asked him to get a ham from the smokehouse to feed some special company who were visiting their family.

He went out to the smokehouse and brought one in. When his mother cut into the meat, he was shocked by the offensive smell and maggots inside the ham. She turned to him and said, "Son, not enough salt, not enough salt."

Kinlaw wrote about how he always remembered the lesson he learned from that ham whenever he heard Jesus' words, "You are the salt of the earth" (Matthew 5:13 NKJ).

He went on to say that you and I live in a society reeking with corruption. Kinlaw said it permeates our culture, the church, and us individually.

"What is the answer?" he asked. "The problem is not that evil is so powerful. It has no power in itself. It only works in the absence of its opposite, and that opposite is holy.

Where the holy reigns, evil can no more exist than maggots can live in salt."

He started me thinking about the struggle between good and evil in every one of us. As a Christian, am I the salt I should be? Could I eliminate some of the rottenness of evil?

The Apostle Paul tells us, "Let your speech always be with grace, seasoned with salt, that you may know how you ought to answer each one" (Colossians 4: 6 NKJV). In Mark 9:50, we read, "Have salt in yourselves, and have peace with one another" (Matthew 5:13 NKJV).

After Jesus said to His followers, "You are the salt of the earth," He then said, "But if the salt loses its flavor, how shall it be seasoned? It is then good for nothing but to be thrown out."

So, are you worth your salt? Just as salt is necessary for good health in our human bodies, we need to be the kind of "salt" necessary to preserve Christian values in our society.

The words of Kinlaw and Burke challenge you and me to take a stand for good and assault evil. It's a task for each of us, beginning with ourselves and those we rub shoulders with.

Who will preserve our society for future generations?

HOW DO YOU AND I KNOW
WHICH WAY WE ARE GOING?

1n 1999, *Time Magazine* called him the "Man of the Century" because he changed science forever.

In 1905, nearly one hundred years earlier, he was a 26-year-old technical officer in a Swiss patent office. He produced three papers that created a new branch of physics. For his first paper, he was awarded a Nobel Prize in 1921.

Albert Einstein was born in Germany in 1879 and attended school in Switzerland where he became a citizen in 1905. When the Nazis seized his property in Germany in 1933, Einstein immigrated to America, accepted a faculty position in Princeton, N.J., and in 1940 became an American citizen.

In his later years, one author described him as a "kindly, absent-minded professor with a wild halo of hair and piercing eyes." His absent-mindedness is illustrated by a story about Einstein traveling on a train one day from his work at Princeton.

The conductor came down the aisle punching the tickets of each passenger. When he came to Einstein, Einstein reached in his vest pocket and couldn't find his ticket. The brilliant scientist looked in his other pocket and it wasn't there. So, he looked in his briefcase and couldn't find it, and it wasn't in the seat by him.

"Dr. Einstein, I know who you are," the conductor said, "We all know who you are. I'm sure you bought a ticket. Don't worry about it." Einstein nodded appreciatively and the conductor continued down the aisle punching tickets.

Just as the conductor was about to move to the next car, he turned around and saw the famous physicist on his hands and knees looking under his seat for his ticket. Rushing back to Einstein, the conductor told him, "Dr. Einstein, don't worry. I know who you are. No problem. You don't need a ticket. I'm sure you bought one."

To which the white-haired professor replied, "Young man, I too know who I am. What I don't know is where I'm going."

Like this brilliant atomic scientist who needed to know where he was going, each of us should ask ourselves, "Do I know where I'm going?" This question needs to be answered spiritually speaking, too.

The Bible says, "There is a way that seems right to a man, but its end is the way of death" (Proverbs 14:12 NKJ). Jesus said that there is a way that leads to destruction and another way that leads to everlasting life.

How do we know if we are going the right way? Jesus simply says, "I am the way, Follow me."

Albert Einstein believed in a "God who reveals Himself in the harmony of all that exists" and that searching for God's design was "the source of all true art and science." God knows who we are and everything about us. We will find Him when we search for Him with all of heart.

READING THE GREATEST LOVE LETTER OF ALL TIME

Years ago, while looking through a collection of old family photos that once belonged to my grandmother, I came across a Whitman's Sampler candy box with cross-stitched flowers printed on it.

Curious, I raised the cover of the cardboard container that time had faded from lemon yellow to a golden honey color. Inside were postcard-size snapshots of grade school classes, family gatherings, and relatives I didn't recognize.

In that box of sweet memories, my grandmother had tucked away a heart-shaped greeting card dated February 13, 1915. She would have been ten-years-old then.

I found it interesting that the Valentine, with its rhyming verse to "the dearest and sweetest girl I know," wasn't signed. Maybe it came from a secret admirer. I can only wonder now.

The tradition of giving Valentines began centuries ago when people wrote their own romantic messages to one another, the earliest dating back to the 1400's. Then, by the early 1800's, hand-painted Valentines decorated with lace and paper flowers were popular in England.

In 1850, Esther Howland, an American artist and printer, was the first to publish and sell Valentines in the United States. The rest is history, as they say. Except for Christmas, more cards are exchanged on Valentine's Day than any other time of year.

A Valentine expresses your love for someone, usually in a few sentimental sentences. The Bible has been described as God's love letter to us. Like a Valentine, verse after verse tells us how much God loves us.

"I have loved thee with an everlasting love," He tells us through the pen of the prophet Jeremiah (31:3 KJV). The apostle Paul was persuaded "that neither death nor life, nor angels nor principalities, nor powers, nor things present, nor things to come, nor height nor depth, nor any other creature, shall be able to separate us from the love of God which is in Christ Jesus our Lord" (Romans 8:38-39 KJV).

John, one of Jesus' disciples, said we love God because He first loved us (1 John 4:19 KJV). God demonstrated His own love toward us in that while we were yet sinners Christ died for us (Romans 5:8 KJV). In the New Testament, we find 1 Corinthians 13, known as the love chapter. John 3:16 tells just how great God loves every one of us, maybe that's why it's sometimes called the heart of the Bible.

An unknown author defined John 3:16 with these details, "For God (the greatest lover) so loved (to the greatest degree) the world (the greatest number) that He gave (the greatest act) His only begotten Son (the greatest gift) that whosoever (the greatest invitation) believeth (the greatest simplicity) in Him (the greatest person) should not perish (the greatest promise) but have (the greatest certainty) everlasting life (the greatest possession)."

Theologian Karl Barth was once asked, "What is the greatest thought you ever had?" He replied, "Jesus loves me this I know, for the Bible tells me so." God is love and it is no secret how much He loves you and me. Just open your Bible and read the greatest love letter of all time.

THE LEGACY OF PATRICK …
5TH CENTURY MISSIONARY

If we could travel back in time and talk to someone from the past, who would you choose?

Hopefully, there would be categories of people to choose from such as presidents, authors, inventors, artists, and others. It would be difficult to select from the men and women of the Bible. But then, we'll have an eternity to talk when the saints go marching in.

A special holiday marks the life of a notable historical figure that would likely be on someone's list, St. Patrick, on March 17. It's the day to wear green, so you won't get pinched. In some big cities, parades march through downtown in his honor.

During a study on the legacy of Patrick several years ago, I learned that this humble 5th century missionary transformed the culture of his day through his devotion to God. Many of his writings have been preserved for us to read.

"I, Patrick, a sinner, a most simple countryman," he begins his personal testimony. Then he tells about his father who was a civil magistrate. Patrick recalls the year A.D. 430 when his hometown in Scotland was attacked by Irish warriors. He writes, "I was taken captive. I was at that time about sixteen years of age. I did not…know the true God; and I was taken into captivity in Ireland with many thousands of people."

Patrick became a slave, forced to tend his master's sheep during six years in bondage, much of that lonely time spent in prayer.

"And there the Lord opened my mind to an awareness

of my unbelief, in order that, even so late, I might remember my transgressions and turn with all my heart to the Lord my God, who had regard for my insignificance and pitied my youth and ignorance. And He watched over me before I knew Him, and before I learned sense or even distinguished between good and evil, and He protected me, and consoled me as a father would his son."

Patrick eventually escaped and returned home, but then went back to Ireland in his mid-40's and travelled on missionary journeys all over pagan Ireland. One of his first converts was his former Master. Patrick spent much of his life ministering in Ireland, training hundreds of pastors and teaching the illiterate.

His ministry brought about a Celtic revival that lasted for almost four centuries. According to historical accounts, Patrick used the shamrock to explain the Trinity. He convinced the Celts to end human sacrifices to their gods and believe in the One who died for all.

Through his devotion to God, Patrick's ministry helped preserve the faith for centuries beyond his lifetime. In Jude 1:3 we read,"…I found it necessary to write to you exhorting you that you to contend earnestly for the faith which was once for all delivered to the saints" (NKJ).

A statement attributed to St. Patrick describes this missionary's life, "I arise today through God's strength to pilot me; God's might to uphold me, God's wisdom to guide me, God's eye to look before me, God's ear to hear me, God's word to speak for me, God's hand to guard me." We are standing on the shoulders of those who have gone before us and we must preserve that legacy of faith for future generations.

SON'S LETTER TO HIS MOTHER
ARE WORDS OF COMFORT TO US

Though you may have never heard of Joseph Scriven, almost everyone has heard the words he wrote in a letter to his mother.

Joseph Scriven was born in 1819 to a prosperous family in Dublin, Ireland and graduated from Trinity College in Dublin. At age 25, he decided to leave his homeland and migrate to Canada – probably because Scriven and his family were estranged. And, sadly, his fiancé accidentally drowned the night before their wedding. So, he went to live in Port Hope, Ontario.

From that time, Scriven's pattern of living changed. He literally lived by the Sermon on the Mount, giving freely of his limited possessions. It is said he never once refused to help anyone who needed it, even sharing his own clothing.

Someone recalled a man who saw Scriven chopping wood and asked about hiring him. He was told, "You can't hire that man; he saws wood only for poor widows and sick people who cannot pay."

Joseph Scriven learned that his mother was seriously ill and he didn't have the money to travel across the ocean to be with her. So, in 1857, he wrote her a letter of comfort, enclosing a poem he titled, "Pray Without Ceasing," as the Bible says in 1 Thessalonians 5:17.

Later, when Scriven himself was ill, a friend came to visit him. The friend noticed the poem scribbled on scratch paper near Joseph's bed. Upon reading it, he asked Scriven if he had written the words. "The Lord and I did between us," was his reply.

Joseph Scriven did not pen his poem for publication. But

his poem found its way into a small collection of hymns and other verses published in 1869.

Then, a talented composer named Charles C. Converse eventually set the poem to music. Ira Sankey, a well-known musician discovered the hymn and it was the last song he added to his hymnal printed in 1875.

Ironically, Joseph Scriven died by accidental drowning in 1886. His words, written over 150 years ago, not only comforted his mother; but millions like you and me still find comfort in the song.

"What a friend we have in Jesus, all our sins and griefs to bear! What a privilege to carry everything to God in prayer! O what peace we often forfeit, O what needless pain we bear, all because we do not carry everything to God in prayer!

"Have we trials and temptations? Is there trouble anywhere? We should never be discouraged. Take it to the Lord in prayer. Can we find a friend so faithful, who will all our sorrows share? Jesus knows our every weakness. Take it to the Lord in prayer.

"Are we weak and heavy laden, cumbered with the load of care? Precious Jesus, still our refuge, take it to the Lord in prayer. Do thy friends despise, forsake thee? Take it to the Lord in prayer; in His arms He'll take and shield thee. Thou wilt find a solace there."

IS THERE A CROSS IN YOUR LIFE?

Two days after the terrorist attacks of 9/11, rescue workers made a remarkable discovery at Ground Zero. Some called it "miracle debris."

On September 13, they found a 20-foot cross made from two steel beams in the crumbled ruins of the World Trade Center. The cross had landed almost upright when the North Tower imploded.

The man who reportedly found the cross cried for twenty minutes after his discovery and the rescue workers prayed and sang "God Bless America" before returning to work.

From that day forward, this cross has touched the lives of many people. News stories told of fire fighters and police officers carving the names of fallen co-workers on it as a way of healing their hurt.

One man who worked during the clean-up said, "The cross bears witness that faith is still here. God gave his Son, his only Son to the people of the world. His Son gave His life for our sins. God hasn't deserted us in this terrible time."

Ironworkers made a pedestal for the cross. It was moved using a crane and placed on a high walkway over a nearby New York street. A Franciscan priest who prayed a prayer of dedication for the massive steel beams on October 4, 2001, stated that this cross symbolized "the pain and suffering of Jesus on the Cross and the redemption of all humanity."

Due to reconstruction in the area, the cross was eventually relocated to St. Peter's Church, which faces the World Trade Center site. A plaque on its pedestal states it will be placed in the WTC Museum, "as a sign of comfort for all."

Someone once said, "The cross is a way of life; the way

of love meeting all hate with love (and) all evil with good."
An English pastor, David Watson, described the Cross of
Christ, "as a picture of violence, yet the key to peace, a
picture of suffering, yet the key to healing, a picture of
death, yet the key to life."

Reading about the cross at Ground Zero reminded me of
Jesus' words to anyone who would believe in Him. "Take
up (your) cross daily, and follow Me" (Luke 9:23 NKJ).

That requires that a person forget about himself or
herself and turn from selfish interests, and, with God's
grace, conform completely to the example of Jesus Christ.
"Christianity is a cross, and a cross is "I" crossed out,"
author and pastor John Bisagno has written.

So, each of us must answer the question, "Is there a cross
in my life?" You may think your life is in shambles, but you
can still come to the cross and find forgiveness and faith. As
one hymn writer put it, "Though millions have come,
there's still room for one. There is room at the cross for you."

From this day forward, you can know true freedom and
forgiveness that only comes from Christ.

IMPORTANT LESSONS LEARNED
FROM SINKING OF TITANTIC

The British luxury liner Titanic was 882.5 feet long, or approximately the length of three football fields. At the time of its maiden voyage in 1912, it was the largest ship ever built. Among the 2,200 people aboard the Titanic were millionaires John Jacob Astor and Isidor Straus, as well as crewmembers and people from all walks of life.

The Titanic sailed from Southampton, England. Its destination was New York City. Around midnight on April 14, the ship struck an iceberg approximately 100 or so miles from Newfoundland and sank in less than three hours.

Since there were only enough lifeboats for half the passenger, acts of courage and cowardice were evident. A Scottish minister, Reverend John Harper, and his daughter were traveling to America to preach at Moody Church in Chicago where he had spoken the year before.

Survivors told how Rev. Harper made certain his six-year-old daughter got into a lifeboat and then he gave his life jacket to another man. During the two hours and 40 minutes the ship was sinking, John Harper was heard shouting, "Let the women, children, and unsaved into the lifeboats."

After the ship sank, a man clinging to a board drifted near Harper in the icy waters. "Are you saved?" Harper pleaded. The man answered, "No."

"Believe on the Lord Jesus Christ and thou shalt be saved," shouted Harper, as the man drifted away without a response. Later, the current brought them near each other again and Reverend Harper cried out, "Are you saved?" Once again, the man said no and Harper repeated the words of Acts 16:31, "Believe on the Lord Jesus Christ and thou shalt be saved."

Though John Harper was one of the 1,517 souls who perished, the man he called out to was rescued and put his faith in Jesus Christ. This survivor testified that he was John Harper's last convert.

Some 705 people were picked up by the ship Carpathia. Another ship nearby did not come to the rescue because its radio operator was off duty and asleep.

Important lessons were learned from this tragedy. Afterwards, every ship had to carry enough lifeboats for every person on board and conduct lifeboat drills. But could there be other lessons we can learn from the Titanic?

For instance, two lists were posted at the Titanic's port in England. One titled, "Lost," listing the names of all those who lost their lives and the other titled, "Saved," listing survivors. No matter who they were – whether wealthy, not so wealthy, officers or crew – each person was either saved or lost.

Some survivors reported hearing the Titanic's band playing the hymn, "Nearer, My God, to Thee" as the ship went down. There's another old hymn that speaks of souls "sinking deep in sin" and lost forever, but there is hope for anyone who believes in the Lord Jesus Christ, who died to save us from our sins.

JESUS HAS NO HANDS BUT YOURS AND MINE

There are certain stories you hear that are so meaningful you never forget them. One that I will always remember comes from a retired military chaplain who shared it with me.

It happened during World War II. After D-Day, our soldiers pushed the Nazis out of France. As each village was liberated, a contingency of GI's was left behind to restore order.

While occupying these towns and cities, they helped the citizens re-establish authority such as local law enforcement. Our armed forces also helped them with the enormous task of cleaning up what the bombing had destroyed.

In a particular town, one of the first buildings the people asked to be repaired was their cathedral. As the pews and altar in the sanctuary were returned to their rightful place, a statue of Jesus was found on the floor.

His hands had been broken off and could not be found in the rubble. While they were trying to decide what to do about replacing Jesus' hands, they put the statue of Him by the altar where it once stood.

One day, the people were amazed at what a soldier had printed on a piece of paper and attached to the statue. It read, "He has no hands, but yours."

It is said that the statue's hands were never replaced and the message with its profound words remains there to this day. The story reminds me of Jesus' words recorded by His disciples.

Our Lord often repeated the phrase, "The kingdom of

heaven is at hand." I know He meant the kingdom of heaven was near, but could there be more significance to the phrase?

I wonder if He was saying we should reach out to those near us, especially those in need, the way He would if He were walking on the earth. Since Christians are His followers, we are His hands. He has no other hands, but ours.

Jesus said when we feed the hungry, clothe those who are naked, or when we visit the sick or those who are in prison, "Insomuch as you have done it unto one of the least of these my brethren, you did it to Me" (Matthew 25:40 KJV).

I've heard it said, "Others will not care how much we know until they know how much we care." There are two questions we need to ask ourselves, "If not me, who? If not now, when?"

William Penn, a Quaker who sailed to America in 1682 and established Philadelphia, the city of brotherly love, once wrote, "I expect to pass through life but once. If, therefore, there be any kindness I can show, or any good thing I can do to any fellow-being, let me do it now, and not defer or neglect it, as I shall not pass this way again."

There are people only an arms-length away from us to whom we can lend a helping hand. You and I must be His hands reaching out to others.

THERE'S AN APP FOR
EVERYTHING YOU NEED IN THE BIBLE

I wonder what Thomas Edison, George Eastman, and Alexander Graham Bell would think if they could see an iPhone or Android phone.

The three famous inventors of a movie camera, Kodak camera, and the telephone would be surprised to see a hand-held electronic device that can record videos, take digital photos, and make phone calls.

Imagine the men's amazement to learn how many applications can be downloaded into a cell phone. By some published reports, there are between 60,000 and 100,000 kinds of applications to download from the internet in categories such as music, cooking, games, work, students, traveling, stocks, and managing money.

If you are cooking, there's an app to set a timer or compile a grocery list. Thousands of recipes can be found via links to websites. You can play scrabble and other educational and entertainment games.

If you enjoy the great outdoors, apps can be downloaded for bird-watching, star-gazing, hiking, biking, running and skiing. You can find maps, a compass, a GPS, and send a panoramic photo of the scenery.

On the small, rectangular screen of a cellular telephone you can "tickle the ivories" on a full 88-key piano with authentic sound. Learn the chords to play a guitar using another app. If you are traveling and do not know the language, there's an app for that too. You can subscribe to apps to stay informed about business, sports, fashion, and much more.

"Apps for everything," Apple advertises on its website.

I've read about new apps available such as a church offering an app for people to download and listen to their services anywhere, anytime. Talk about preaching the Gospel outside the four walls of the sanctuary.

Several publishers have introduced apps to download the Bible, study helps, commentaries, and Bible quizzes. I see more and more people during worship services reading the Scripture on their cell phones as the pastor reads his sermon text. There's no other book like the Bible with "apps for everything." In God's inspired Word with its 31,103 verses, you can find applications for everything you need to know.

The Bible provides a moral compass and GPS (God's Plan for Salvation). Need a map? "The Bible is God's chart for you to steer by," Henry Ward Beecher once wrote. Planning a budget? Read Mark 4 and Luke 19. Participating in sports? Turn to 2 Timothy 2:5. If you're starting a new job, go to Psalm 1, Proverbs 16, and Philippians 3:7-21.

Want to know the recipe for a good marriage and parenting children? You'll find apps for every relationship. The Bible has been called food for the soul. Are you sick or in pain? Read Psalms 6, 29, 41, 67; and Isaiah 26. Are you lonely or fearful? Search for Psalm 27, Psalm 91, Luke 8 and 1 John 3.

Author Keith Miller has written, "The Bible can change not only a life, but an entire lifestyle." Read it again and again to find the Truth to apply to your life!

400TH ANNIVERSARY OF THE BOOK THAT CHANGED THE WORLD

The King James Bible, the best-selling book of all time, reached a milestone in 2011. Special events were planned to celebrate the 400th anniversary of the KJV's publication in 1611.

The Sunday Times of London reports that King James saw "his task as giving his newly acquired kingdom a beautiful gift that would also serve as a unifying force," having been persuaded by the Puritans that a new translation of the Bible was needed.

Puritans sought to simplify and regulate forms of worship. When the Pilgrims, those Puritans who felt persecuted by the established church, decided to leave England to start a new life in the New World, they took the King James Bible with them.

The King James Bible Trust, organizers of the anniversary events, describes the KJ Bible as the book that changed the world. "British sailors took the Bible on voyages around the globe; Through the work of the East India Company it was taken to India and to the colonies in Africa, Australia and New Zealand. This is one reason why English is now a world language," according to www.kingjamesbibletrust.org.

In 1777, Congress voted to import 20,000 copies of the Bible from Scotland because shipments from England were cut off during the Revolutionary War. The Bible was the basis for religion, education, and colonial government.

Our sixth president John Quincy Adams once said, "The first and almost the only Book deserving of universal attention is the Bible." President Calvin Coolidge has written, "The foundations of our society and our government rest so much on the teachings of the Bible that it would be difficult to support them if faith in these teachings would cease to be practically universal in our country."

Another reason the King James Bible changed the world is summed up by Andrew Motion, Poet Laureate of the United Kingdom 1999-2009. "The King James Bible is a cornerstone of our culture and our language. Whatever our faith, whatever we believe, we have to recognize that the rhetorical power of this book, and in particular its power to fuse history with poetry, connects at the most fundamental level with our own history and poetry."

Many words and phrases we use today come from the King James Bible. Have you ever called someone the "salt of the earth"? You've quoted from the KJV. To "turn the other cheek" or want an "eye for an eye" and many other familiar phrases come from the KJV.

The YouTube Bible is an "ambitious project to create a complete reading of the King James Bible on YouTube." People around the world are welcomed to contribute one chapter or several chapters.

The King James Bible, translated from Hebrew and Greek manuscripts by six groups of scholars, gave us an English version of the Word of God, which is "quick, and powerful....a discerner of the thoughts and intents of the heart" (Hebrews 4:12 KJV). It's a book that continues to change my life because God's inspired words teach eternal Truth.

LIFE WITHOUT GOD
WOULD BE UNIMAGINABLE

What I know about using a computer makes me feel like a first grader attempting to study an encyclopedia. The more I learn about these electronic machines, the more I realize how much there is to learn. Yet, I can't imagine life without computers.

For instance, typing on a computer helps me write this column. The computer displays my words on a monitor like a television screen, instead of a blank sheet of paper in a typewriter. With a word processing program, I can ask the computer to check my spelling and punctuation, something a typewriter could never do. Word processing also saves me a lot of time because I can rearrange words and sentences without retyping an entire page.

The development of computer technology has created new terminology resulting in a language of its own. For a computer novice like me, learning computer terms has taught me new definitions to familiar words.

A sacred, religious statue called an icon can also represent a symbol for a computer function like edit, print or search. A terminal is not just a place to board a bus, train, or airplane; it's also a word for a monitor and/or keyboard connected to one main computer.

I've always heard that a long day of traveling was a hard drive, now it can be the mechanical part of the computer where information can be stored and retrieved. You could compare a computer to an electronic filing cabinet that can store more information than a room full of filing cabinets.

Sometimes I've wondered what the Apostle Paul, John Wesley or King James translators would think if they could know that 1,000 plus pages of the Bible can be found on a drive the size of a finger. Imagine their amazement if they could see a computer search for a particular verse and find it in a few seconds.

I've found what I think are some Biblical applications of computer terms. There's an essential key on the computer keyboard usually found in the upper left-hand corner. It's labeled "ESC" for escape and allows me to go to another screen or file when necessary.

This reminds me of the Apostle Paul's words concerning temptation when he said God will not allow more than you can bear, "…. but with the temptation will also make a way of escape" for you and me (1 Corinthians 10:13 NKJ).

We find ourselves daily logging onto the Internet. This network allows access to unlimited resources of information on the web pages or websites of schools, businesses, organizations, and individuals.

We are now seeing a glimpse of the evangelism outreach to the world through this electronic mission field. When Jesus chose his disciples, He said, "Follow me, and I will make you fishers of men" (Mathew 4:19 KJV). The disciples could not have imagined a "net" so large the Gospel of Jesus Christ could be spread around the world instantly 24 hours a day.

Like the time-saving computer, there's much to learn about our soul-saving God. He wants us to know about Him by reading the pages of His Word. But there's no way our finite minds can know everything about our infinite God. According to the Apostle Paul, God is "able to do exceedingly abundantly above all we ask or think…" (Ephesians 3:20 NKJ). And I can't imagine life without Him.

WHAT I LEARNED ABOUT MAMA FROM HER BIBLES

"We want you to go through Mama's Bibles," an uncle requested several years ago when my husband's grandmother passed away.

The family faced the sad task of deciding what to do with her precious possessions. Among them were three Bibles…a large print King James with a dusty rose leather binding, a small black one with her name engraved on the front corner, and a third one with "Holy Bible" in giant, gold letters on the cover.

During her 88 years of life, Thelma Boothe not only read her Bible, she also put memories within its pages. A dozen or more pieces of paper in the Holy Bible with giant letters made it almost twice its thickness.

Tenderly, I turned each page to see what she had saved or written. Being known as the family historian granted me the privilege of determining any information that needed to be preserved. What I found told me more about my grandmother by marriage.

Mama Boothe, as we called her, filled her Bibles with newspaper clippings, now yellowed by time. Some were photos of her children's and grandchildren's accomplishments and celebrations. The newspaper clippings announced weddings, school awards, and job recognitions. Happy events included a family member's 50th anniversary and another's record-breaking cucumber.

There were at least two columns by Ann Landers, one on the high cost of alcoholism and another titled, "First to forgive is the first to find peace." She had also kept an article written by a local minister about "that old time religion."

Between the pages were bookmarks of all descriptions…a Christmas ribbon, a crocheted cross, and a paper cross that read "Happy Mother's Day." Many other clippings told of the deaths of relatives and friends whom she knew and loved during her lifetime. I found her mother's obituary dated July 1965.

Mama wrote in the margins and back cover of her Bible. "There was a hailstorm the 26th day of March in 1983, biggest one I ever saw," she jotted inside the cover. She noted the passing of her sister-in-law Pearl, who was 92-years-old.

What touched my heart most were comments about Scriptures. On the page beside Psalm 91, she wrote, "Brent and I read this chapter often to Big Mama White (my husband's paternal grandmother). Numerous verses were underlined, some with a minister's name in the margin marking a sermon she probably heard.

Even though she didn't say much about her walk with God, I was holding the foundation of her faith. As I reached the last page of her Bible, I thought about the end of her life. A couple of days before she died, she said, "I'm ready to go to heaven."

Looking back on her life, I was reminded of a verse the Apostle Paul wrote to a young man named Timothy, "When I call to remembrance the genuine faith…which dwelt first in your grandmother Lois and your mother Eunice," and I am persuaded it is in you also (2 Timothy 1:5 NKJ). The Apostle Paul was telling him to keep the faith. I pray the same will be true of me.

WHO CAN MEASURE THE VALUE
OF A GODLY MOTHER?

A minister was talking to a mischievous five-year-old boy, "So your mother says your prayers with you each night? Wonderful! What does she say?" The little boy replied, "Thank God he's in bed!"

Charles Swindoll, an author and minister, describes a great big Mother's Day card he once read. On the front, there was a picture of a small boy with a tiny cut on his face, his sneakers untied. The youngster was pulling a wagon. Toys were everywhere.

The card read, "Mom, I remember that little prayer you used to say for me every day." Inside, it said, "God help you if you ever do that again."

"Nothing else will ever make you as happy or as sad, as proud or as tired, as motherhood," writes Elia Parsons, co-author of *The Mother's Almanac*. How well I remember the joy I felt the first time I held our daughter in my arms. The diaper days and school days that I thought would last forever seemed to pass all too quickly. Now she is grown up.

There's one thing I've been doing almost every day since the day she was born. I've prayed for Kelley. I will continue to ask God to bless her, and guide her, and keep her safe - just as my mother still prays for me.

"As a mother, my job is to take care of the possible and trust God with the impossible," Ruth Bell Graham once said. Her husband puts it this way, "Only God Himself fully appreciates the influence of a Christian mother in the molding of character in her children."

If you're ever tempted to doubt the importance of

motherhood, just remember the words of William Ross Wallace. "The hand that rocks the cradle is the hand that rules the world."

Consider these examples of two presidents and the founder of the Methodist Church.

Our first president, George Washington, stated, "All I am I owe to my mother. I attribute all my success in life to the moral, intellectual and physical education I received from her."

Abraham Lincoln said, "I remember my mother's prayers and they have always followed me. They have clung to me all my life." He reminds us, "No man is poor who had a godly mother."

"I learned more about Christianity from my mother than from all the theologians of England," John Wesley recalled. Nineteen children were born to Susanna and Samuel Wesley between 1690 and 1709 (only nine lived into adulthood). John was her 15th child. He and his brother, Charles, founded the Methodist Church.

Two months before she died, John preached a series of revival messages to the biggest crowds his hometown had ever seen. Susanna's prayers for her children made an impact for generations to come.

The value of a godly mother can be measured when "her children rise up, and call her blessed" (Proverbs 31:28 NKJ).

RESTRAINT IS IMPORTANT
LESSON IN LIFE

The first thing I do when I get in my car is reach over my left shoulder, pull the seat belt across my body and fasten the metal clip in the slot. I don't want to drive until the click tells me I'm secure.

I admit I haven't always buckled up. Like others who don't wear them, I had my excuses years ago. I used to say seat belts were uncomfortable and too confining. They wrinkle my clothes, I'd complain. Or I'd be in a hurry and never think about the safety factor.

I let my excuses overrule the fact I know seat belts save lives. You've probably heard the crash statistics. For instance, during a typical year almost half the people killed in car or truck accidents are not wearing seat belts.

Seat belt usage in Alabama has reportedly increased to 97%, largely as a result of Alabama's primary restraint law and the Click It or Ticket enforcement and education campaigns.

I started buckling up, not just because it is a state law, but also because I heard about a minister's personal experience. His car was hit from behind at an intersection while waiting for a red light. He said he would have been killed if he had not been wearing his seat belt.

He made a believer out of me. Since then, I feel like something's missing if I don't buckle up. Not feeling the restraint of the seat belt makes me feel unprotected in my car. What used to feel confining is now comforting.

There's a lesson to be learned about restraint, spiritually speaking. We live in a society that doesn't seem to want any restraint; and I'm not just talking about people who refuse to wear their seat belt. There's an obvious lack of moral restraint that threatens the safety of our society.

Author Ron Mehl's book, titled *The Ten(der) Commandments,* says the Ten Commandments are often portrayed as ominous warnings instead of ten declarations of God's love for us.

He writes, "Have you ever heard of the ten commandments described as a love letter... a tender, heartfelt message from the very hand of God? Perhaps not. Yet, I've become convinced it is one of the most powerful expressions of God's love in all of Scripture."

For example, when God said, "Thou shalt not steal" (Exodus 20:15), He was not just warning thieves; but He was protecting the rest of us from having something valuable stolen by them.

God commanded, "Thou shalt not commit adultery" (Exodus 20:14), not just to forbid illicit relationships, but because He knew its destructiveness to marriages and hurt that impacts children whose parents divorce. Immorality of any kind puts a person at risk for dangerous diseases.

"Every law that God has given has been for man's benefit. If man breaks it, he is not only rebelling against God, he is hurting himself," Billy Graham once said. Loving God means keeping his commandments. And His commandments are not burdensome. His Word promises, "Keep my commands and live." (Proverbs 7:2 NKJ)

YOU AND I CAN BE ADOPTED
AS CHILDREN IN THE FAMILY OF GOD

What do Alexander the Great, George Washington Carver, Art Linkletter, Eleanor Roosevelt, John Lennon and Steve Jobs have in common? All of them were adopted.

Authors Louisa May Alcott, Charles Dickens, Edgar Allen Poe, and James Michener were involved in adoptions.

Aristotle tops the list, as well as John J. Audubon. Included are actresses such as Melissa Gilbert and Marilyn Monroe, and politicians like President Gerald Ford, President Bill Clinton, and Nelson Mandela who were adoptees.

Singers Nat King Cole, Ella Fitzgerald, Faith Hill, and Sarah McLachlan are listed. Football player/commentator Tim Green and former # 2 rusher in the NFL Eric Dickerson, along with baseball Hall of Famer Jim Palmer and Olympic figure skater Scott Hamilton were all raised by someone other than their birth parents.

One of the best-known adoptees in recent years founded a fast-food restaurant chain called Wendy's. Dave Thomas was adopted by a couple in Kalamazoo, Michigan at the age of six months. In 1992, he created a foundation with the vision that "every child will have a permanent home and a loving family." His organization focuses on increasing adoption awareness.

I once heard Lee Ezell share her personal experience. After suffering from a brutal rape, Lee discovered she was pregnant. A young, single person, she bravely chose to place her child for adoption. Twenty years later, Lee was shocked to hear a voice on the other end of the telephone say, "Hi, I'm Julie and you're my mother." Julie has said, "I am so thankful to have been loved and adopted by a special family, but to also have the opportunity to know and grow to love my birth mother."

Adoption is defined as a legal process by which people take as their own a child who was not born to them. I've read that adopted children are entitled to the same privileges as children born to parents, including the right to inherit property.

Ever since the earliest days of mankind, families have been formed through adoption. In fact, we read about adoption in the Bible. We read in Exodus chapter two about an Egyptian princess adopting a Hebrew baby and hiring his mother to take care of him. Moses (that was his Egyptian name) was raised in Pharaoh's household.

A young girl named Esther who had no parents was adopted by her cousin Mordecai. You can read her story in the book of Esther. She later became Queen of Persia.

According to Unger's Bible dictionary, adoption is also a theological term for an act of God whereby a repentant sinner is made a member of the family of God, as if he had been born in the family with all the rights and privileges of a child.

The Apostle Paul writes that Jesus was born and died "to redeem us that we might receive the adoption" as his sons and daughters (Galatians 4:4-6 KJV). We can be born again into the family of God through Christ's sacrifice for the forgiveness of our sins.

STAND UP FOR
YOUR COUNTRY AND GOD

There are special people you meet through the years who make a lasting impression on your life. I will never forget meeting Colonel Jerry Sage, a World War II veteran, who retired in Enterprise, Alabama. He was recognized as Enterprise "Man of the Year" in 1991.

Many years ago, Sage was speaking to a local group of Civitans about his extraordinary military experiences and, in doing so, made some thought-provoking comments regarding religion and politics.

He gave God the credit for helping him accomplish heroic deeds and surviving brutal torture during World War II. "So many things happened to me," said the old soldier. That was an understatement.

Sage told of his experiences as a guerrilla leader and saboteur with the OSS (Office of Strategic Services), the forerunner of the CIA. His code name was "Dagger" because it was the only weapon he carried with him.

Using explosives and detonating devices, he and his men would blow tanks and other military equipment, as well as bridges, behind Nazi lines in North Africa. He was shot and stabbed numerous times, in addition to having his nose broken six times.

The retired colonel said he still suffered back pain due to German guards kicking him with their boots. He told of escaping his German captors eight times. Each time Sage was recaptured, he spent weeks in solitary confinement where he earned the nickname, "Cooler King."

"When you're alone in a cinder block room and given one potato a day, you'll talk to God," Sage recalled. At

Stalag 13, Sage and other POW's dug tunnels beneath the camp where he devised a plan to hide tons of sand. In 1963, a movie was made about Sage and his men called, "The Great Escape," starring Steve McQueen as Capt. Hilts, based on Sage's experiences.

Colonel Sage told Civitans that he would go through all his war experiences again to defend his country. The veteran concluded his speech with a statement about religion and politics that I still take to heart.

Though there's an old saying about not mixing the two topics, I find that religion – or the faith given once for all (see Jude 3) - impacts every area of my life as a wife, mother, and writer. It's more than church attendance on Sunday.

When a candidate or party supports issues that go against Biblical principles, I cannot support them. As a citizen and a Christian who believes in the sanctity of life and marriage between a man and woman, I must stand up for what I believe is Truth. I vote these core values by researching for myself the candidate's record, not just what he or she says.

I pay my debt of gratitude to those who have fought and died for our freedom by exercising my privilege to vote. It's also important to ask God for wisdom before going to the polls.

I can still hear Colonel Sage's challenge, "People say, 'Don't talk about religion and politics.' Well, your politics is your country and religion is about your God. Stand up and be counted on both."

YOU ARE WRITING YOUR OBITUARY EACH DAY

In 1897, Mark Twain sent the following note to the London correspondent of the *New York Journal*, "The report of my death is greatly exaggerated."

I've heard it said, "If you get up in the morning and you don't read your obituary in the newspaper, it's a good day." Of course, it is said in jest, but think about it. Each new day is a gift from God. "This is the day the Lord has made," the Psalmist wrote (118:24 NKJ).

One morning in 1888, a Swedish chemist named Alfred Nobel, the inventor of dynamite who amassed a fortune from the manufacture of weapons, awoke to read his obituary in the newspaper.

Alfred's brother had died and a French reporter mistakenly wrote the obituary about the wrong brother. Nobel was not only disturbed by the error; he was shocked to read how his life would be remembered.

"The dynamite king," as his obituary stated, was also described "as a great industrialist who made an immense wealth from explosives." As far as the public was concerned, this was the entire purpose of his life.

His true intentions had always been to break down the barriers that separated men and ideas, yet he would only be remembered as a merchant of death. As he read his obituary, Nobel determined the world would know the true meaning and purpose of his life.

Alfred Nobel decided his last will and testament regarding his wealth would show the world his intentions. He set up a fund of about $9 million, specifying how the interest from the money would be used.

Annual prizes were to be awarded to people whose work had to have benefited humanity. He died in 1896 and the first Nobel prizes were awarded in 1901. A medal and a cash award are given in five categories – physics and chemistry, physiology or medicine, literature, peace and economics.

Every morning we should be thankful to be alive. We have another day of life and breath to make the world a better place in which to live. Helen Keller once said, "I will not just live my life. I will not just spend my life. I will invest my life." Or, in the words of theologian Matthew Henry, "It ought to be the business of every day to prepare for our last day." A minister friend once said, "We live in ever-dying bodies with a never-dying soul."

There's a song, written by Don Moen, that's been on my mind this week because my Dad is critically ill. "When it's all been said and done, there is just one thing that matters. Did I do my best to live for truth? Did I live my life for you?

"When it's all been said and done, all my treasures will mean nothing. Only what I have done for love's rewards will stand the test of time…. I will always sing your praise here on earth and in heaven after for you've joined me at my true home. When it's all been said and done, you're my life when life is gone."

CANADIAN OVERCOMES ADVERSITY TO IMPACT THE WORLD

The fourth child of Scottish immigrants was born in Ramsay Township in Ontario, Canada on November 6, 1861. By age 9, Jim had lost both of his parents. His grandmother raised him until her death two years later. Then, he lived with a bachelor uncle.

In 1875, Jim entered high school, but attended less than two years. Later, he did complete his high school equivalency in a year and a half, graduating in 1883. Then, he attended McGill University in Montreal where he earned a Bachelor of Arts in Physical Education; participating in football, rugby, and lacrosse. Jim often visited the YMCA in Montreal.

The young man went on to receive a Master's degree in 1890 from the Presbyterian College of Theology in Montreal. During a rugby game his senior year, a player on his team uttered some profanity, apologizing to Jim by saying "I forgot you were there." Those words changed Jim's life and gave him the idea to help men through physical and spiritual development.

Jim chose not to go into the ministry, but instead came to Springfield, Massachusetts to serve as a PE instructor at the YMCA's International Training School for Christian Workers "to win men for the Master through the gym."

In those days, indoor physical education consisted of calisthenics, gymnastics, and drills. Participation in outdoor sports like football and track and field at the YMCA was on the increase. Luther Gulick, Jim' supervisor, asked him to invent new games for students to play indoors during the winter months.

Jim remembered a game he played as a child called "duck-on-a-rock," in which players threw a rock at a "duck" placed on top of a large rock, trying to knock the "duck" off. So, he nailed peach baskets for goals on the wall at each end of the gym floor, and a soccer ball for players to pass as teams ran back and forth between the baskets. No tackles were allowed.

In 1891, James "Jim" Naismith invented the game of basketball. Jim replaced the peach baskets with iron hoops and a hammock-style basket. The open-ended nets like we use today came ten years later.

In his book, *Basketball: Its Origin and Development*, published after his death, Naismith wrote, "Whenever I witness games in a church league, I feel that my vision, almost half a century ago, of the time when the Christian people would recognize the true value of athletics, has become a reality."

"Be strong in body, clean in mind, lofty in ideals," James Naismith once said. Maybe he taught athletes how to achieve these three with the scripture, "I can do all things through Christ who strengthens me" (Philippians 4:13 KJV).

Interestingly enough, Jim never profited from the game he invented and did not accept any fees when speaking about basketball. He and his wife, Maude, had five children. Naismith died of a heart attack in 1939. He left a legacy of faith and the gift of a game played in more than 200 countries around the world.

DON'T BE AFRAID OF
THE 'UNS' OF LIFE

Although I've flown many times, I still face the fear factor when it comes to flying. Fear doesn't keep me grounded because I know about the "uns" of life -- the "uns" that the airlines tell you about and the "uns" that God wants you to know.

Once passengers find their assigned seats before a flight, a stewardess begins making announcements. During this brief information session, passengers are told what to do in case of emergency.

In the unlikely event the cabin loses air pressure, an oxygen mask will drop down from the compartment above your head. The stewardess holds a mask and shows how the elastic band fits around your head and the mask covers your nose and mouth.

Passengers are instructed to keep their seatbelts fastened while they're seated in case of unexpected turbulence. Whether the flight will travel over land or sea, you learn your seat cushion can be used as a flotation device.

Get the picture? The airlines want passengers to know what to do should the unlikely and unexpected happen. Often, the problems we encounter in life are considered unlikely because they are unexpected, unwanted and usually come unannounced.

With each new day, we face "uns" because life is unpredictable. Ever notice the word "if" is in the center of the word, life? The future is uncertain and unknown. From time to time, every one of us will encounter turbulence. Winds of adversity can make life a bumpy journey.

We do not know from day to day when unforeseen

circumstances may find us, or a family member, battling an illness or undergoing surgery. Some accidents are unavoidable. A financial crisis may catch us unaware. Unfaithfulness unravels family ties.

During those times, remember we serve a God whose love and power are unlimited. He is unchanging. He's the same "yesterday, today, and forever" (Hebrews 13:8 NKJ). When things seem uncontrollable to us, remember that God is in control.

The Bible says, "Lean not on your own understanding" (Proverbs 3:5b NKJ). I do not understand aerodynamics and how huge jet planes, loaded with lots of people get off the ground and soar into the air, traveling miles above the earth.

Likewise, I do not understand when bad things happen to good people. But when the unthinkable occurs, I do know that the peace that God gives me surpasses all my understanding.

When a passenger boards an airplane, they don't sit in the cockpit. They trust that the pilot's skill and the plane's radar will get them to their destination. Let God be your pilot in life. He knows all and sees all from His eternal vantage point. Fear causes us to carry excess baggage around with us that we weren't meant to carry. Let go and let God unburden you of whatever weighs you down.

We don't know what may happen today, tomorrow, next week, next month, next year, or during our lifetimes. But we can live unafraid because we know the One who holds the future. We can trust Him to be with us through the journey of life and, in His time, carry us to our eternal destination in heaven.

COACH WON SOULS FOR CHRIST & RECORD NUMBER OF GAMES

On any given Fall or Winter Sunday, NFL teams line up to compete. Will we see an onside kick, an end-around, a double reverse, or maybe the flea-flicker?

All these football plays have one thing in common. They originated with a coach named Amos Alonzo Stagg. He also introduced the basic principles of the T-formation and invented the tackling dummy, as well as numbered jerseys, huddles, and athletic letters.

Stagg won 314 games during his coaching career at the University of Chicago (1892-1932) and the College of the Pacific (1933-1946). Only a few coaches have won more games – including Paul Bryant and Eddie Robinson.

Born in West Orange, NJ in 1862, Stagg's devotion to hard work made him successful in the classroom and athletic field. He also grew in his spiritual disciplines and, acting on the guidance of his pastor, Sunday School teacher and sister, Stagg enrolled at Yale to become a Presbyterian minister.

In college, he excelled in baseball and football and was selected for the very first All-American Team in 1889. Stagg received lucrative offers from professional baseball clubs, but he still wanted to become a pastor. Though he had no problem living his faith, when speaking in front of large groups he would struggle to express his faith.

Instead of the ministry, Amos Alonzo Stagg decided to pursue a coaching career. His first job out of college in 1888 was head football coach at the School of Christian Workers, a YMCA training school in Springfield, Massachusetts.

The center of his offensive line was none other than

James Naismith, who shared with him his own ideas for a new game called basketball. A scheduling conflict prevented Stagg from playing in that sport's first game.

When approached about the head-coaching position at the University of Chicago, he replied, "After much thought and prayer, I decided that my life can best be used for my Master's service in the position you have offered."

His success has been attributed to his lofty expectations on and off the field. He looked at football as a great endeavor in developing biblical manhood, demanding from his players hard work, intense focus, and sacrifice for his team.

"Win the athletes at any college for Christ," Stagg once said, "and you will have the strongest working element attainable in college life." He saw every missed field goal as a test of faith and every clash on the line of scrimmage as a test of character. He believed that teamwork developed bonds of Christ-like love and prepared souls to receive the Gospel.

Amos Alonzo Stagg's teams dominated the Big Ten for twenty years. He coached until he was 98-years-old, compiling a record of 314-199-35. In 1965, he died at the age of 103.

I can imagine hearing Coach Stagg teaching his teams the words of the Apostle Paul who said, "I press toward the goal for the prize of the upward call of God in Christ Jesus" (Philippians 3:14 NJV).

CONVINCING PROOF
OF CHRIST'S RESURRECTION

Suppose someone questioned the fact of Christ's resurrection from the grave after His death by crucifixion. How would you answer?

You could reply with the Apostle Paul's list of those who saw the risen Lord, including Peter, the twelve, and "over five hundred brethren at once" (1 Corinthians 15:6 NKJ). Then, to complicate matters, the person refuses to accept the Bible's eyewitness accounts. How would you make a convincing case to prove the resurrection of Jesus Christ?

In his book, *Loving God,* Charles Colson makes the case for Christ's resurrection based on his Watergate experience. Names like John Dean, Bob Haldeman, and Colson are remembered for their involvement in the scandal that forced President Nixon to resign in 1972.

Chuck Colson, who was convicted for obstruction of justice, wrote about his role in the cover-up in *Loving God.* He recalled the burglary of the office in the Watergate building of the National Democratic Committee and the investigation of Nixon administration officials.

Colson told of John Dean contacting prosecutors to "bargain his testimony for immunity." The cover-up conspiracy was discovered. "With the most powerful office in the world at stake, a small band of hand-picked loyalists, no more than ten of us, could not hold a conspiracy together for more than two weeks," Colson points out.

But what does Watergate have to do with the resurrection of Jesus? Colson cited the accusation that the apostles removed Christ's body from the tomb (Matthew 28:13 KJV). Even 2,000 years ago, there were some who refused to believe the resurrection.

Based on his Watergate experience, Colson believes there couldn't have been a conspiracy because 11 men wouldn't have defended a lie with their lives. Each of them kept telling about Christ's life, death, and resurrection to anyone who would listen, until their last breath.

Church historians record that Peter was killed by crucifixion. He requested to be executed upside down, considering himself unworthy to be crucified the same as Christ. Andrew was also crucified. He hung for two days praising God and telling spectators to believe. James was slain with a sword by Herod.

Colson states, "Take it from one who was inside the Watergate web looking out, who saw firsthand how vulnerable a cover-up is: Nothing less… (than the witness of Someone) …as awesome as the resurrected Christ could have caused those men to maintain to their dying whispers that Jesus is alive and Lord."

There have always been doubters. Maybe you have questioned the authenticity of Jesus' resurrection. If so, consider accepting for yourself the evidence that led Colson to his belief that, "This weight of evidence tells me the apostles were indeed telling the truth: Jesus did rise bodily from the grave, He is who He says He is."

Not only is the truth of Christ's resurrection worth dying for, it's worth living for. As the hymn writer put it, "Because He lives, I can face tomorrow… (and I find) life is worth the living, just because He lives."

GET RID OF YOUR LUMBER BEFORE YOU REMOVE OTHER'S SPLINTERS

Sometimes you read something that gives you food for thought. I read a quote attributed to Holocaust survivor Corrie Ten Boom that's given me a plateful to digest.

"When a Christian shuns fellowship with other Christians, the devil smiles. When he stops studying the Bible, the devil laughs. When he stops praying, the devil shouts for joy."

Someone once said, "If the church were perfect, you could not belong" and neither could I. There are no perfect churches because there are no perfect people.

A thought-provoking article on the front of a church bulletin told of a minister who kept a special notebook on his desk at the church. On the cover of the notebook were these words, "Complaints of Members Against Other Members."

When someone would tell the minister the faults of another person, he would say, "Here's my complaint book. I'll write down what you say, and you can sign it. Then when I have to take the matter up with the brethren, I will know what testimony to expect from you."

Seeing the open notebook and pen on his desk always had its effect. "Oh no! I couldn't sign anything like that!" the member would respond. No one would want to put his or her complaints in writing.

The story concluded with the minister telling that he'd kept the complaint book for over 40 years, and had opened it thousands of times, but had never had occasion to write a single word in it.

His experience reminds me of a statement I've heard

people make through the years. When you point a finger at someone else, there are three pointing back at you. It's been said that if you feel constrained to look for faults, use a mirror, not a telescope.

Jesus talked about "complaints" in Matthew chapter seven, verse one. He said, "Judge not, that ye be not judged" (KJV). Then He went on to say that you and I will be judged according to the way we judge others.

If you will permit me to paraphrase, Jesus also said we see the splinter in another person's eye and don't see the two-by-four in our own eye. In other words, you have to get rid of your own lumber before you can see clearly enough to get the splinter out of your fellow Christian's eye.

Should someone commit a sin that needs to be addressed, Jesus gave us guidelines in Matthew 18 beginning in verse 15. He said to go to the person privately first. If the person refuses to listen to you, then take another Christian with you and speak privately to them again. If all else fails, take the matter up with the church.

When we are tempted to complain about others, we could learn from the wise words of an elderly minister I know. Since God gave us two ears and one mouth, maybe we should only talk half as much as we listen.

The best rule of thumb is to remember, if you can't be big, don't belittle.

IN SEARCH OF SANCTUARY

Though I've attended services in many different churches during my lifetime, there's something special about entering any sanctuary that I find hard to describe.

No matter the location and size of the church, the building has a sacred atmosphere. From the majestic marble and granite National Cathedral in Washington, D.C. to the white clapboard Lambeth Chapel at Blue Lake Methodist Camp in south Alabama, there's a sense of awe and reverence in these houses of worship.

Standing at the back of the sanctuary, one typically sees row after row of wooden pews. The carpeted aisle leads straight towards the altar, a place of prayer just the right height for kneeling.

A pulpit usually stands on a wide platform, higher than the rest of the sanctuary, where the minister speaks to the congregation. Behind the pulpit, there's often a choir loft with pews or chairs on still higher levels.

A sanctuary is special, not because of its furnishings, though they provide a comfortable place for worship. A sanctuary is special because people go there to meet with God. Maybe that's why we sometimes call a church the "house of God."

It's important that we attend church. God instructs us in His word about the importance of believers coming together, especially on the Lord's Day. Hebrews 10:25 instructs us about "Not forsaking the assembling of ourselves together" as is the habit of some people (NKJ).

But what about meeting with God the other days of the week? We can meet with God on a daily basis by spending time in prayer and reading His word. Another definition for sanctuary is a place of refuge, a shelter for protection or a safe haven.

Have you ever needed that kind of sanctuary? I search for it – a quiet time away from the hectic pace of life. Surprisingly, I've found sanctuary in the rather mundane places of everyday life.

Sometimes my car becomes a sanctuary. While sitting in the driver's seat behind the steering wheel, I tell God my prayer requests for that day or sing a hymn of praise to Him.

At times, I've found sanctuary just standing at the sink washing dishes. I may be up to my elbows in soapsuds, but I talk to God about what's on my mind.

There's a particular chair in my home where I like to kneel and pray, while other times I bow beside my bed. These become sacred places where I reach heaven on my knees.

Find sanctuary by attending the church of your choice. Get into the habit of spending time with God, one on one each day. Search for your personal sanctuary. God will meet you there.

LEAVING BEHIND FOOTPRINTS IN THE SANDS OF TIME

"That's one small step for man, one giant leap for mankind." Apollo 11 Commander Neil Armstrong spoke those famous words on July 20, 1969 upon taking his first step on the moon.

Forty years ago, astronauts Buzz Aldrin, Michael Collins and Armstrong traveled 231,800 miles from the earth to the moon in three days. After their space craft entered the lunar orbit, Armstrong and Aldrin descended in the lunar module - the Eagle - landing on the moon.

Reportedly, more than half a billion people watched on television as Armstrong climbed down the ladder and put his left foot on the moon. Aldrin set foot on the moon fifteen minutes after Armstrong. They explored the lunar surface for two and a half hours, collecting samples of rocks, as well as taking photographs.

They left behind an American flag and a plaque that read, "Here men from the planet Earth first set foot upon the moon. July 1969 A.D. We came in peace for all mankind." Over the next three and a half years, ten astronauts followed in their footsteps – one of the last was Gene Cernan, commander of the final Apollo mission.

I found it interesting that, according to NASA, the footprints on the moon will be there for a million years because there is no wind to blow them away. As Henry Wadsworth Longfellow has written, "Lives of great men all remind us we can make our lives sublime. And, departing, leave behind us footprints in the sands of time."

Someone once said, "The footprints you leave behind will influence others. There is no person who at some time, somewhere, somehow, does not lead another." 1 Peter 2:21 reminds each of us that Christ walked on planet earth, "leaving you an example that you should follow in his steps" (NIV). The apostle Paul wanted to live his life so that anyone who followed him, followed Christ (1 Corinthians 11:1).

There's a song whose words speak of the footprints we should leave behind. "We're pilgrims on the journey of the narrow road and those who've gone before us line the way, cheering on the faithful, encouraging the weary - their lives a stirring testament to God's sustaining grace....as those who've gone before us, let us leave to those behind us the heritage of faithfulness passed on through godly lives.

"After all our hopes and dreams have come and gone and our children sift through all we've left behind may the clues that they discover and the memories they uncover become the light that leads them to the road we each must find.

"Oh, may all who come behind us find us faithful may the fire of our devotion light their way may the footprints that we leave lead them to believe and the lives we live inspire them to obey. Oh, may all who come behind us find us faithful."

When we depart from life in this world, what kind of prints will you and I leave behind?

PRESERVE THE PRECIOUS MEMORIES OF YOUR FAMILY

Summertime is the season for family reunions and church homecoming celebrations. These special events provide the perfect time and place to reminisce.

Traditionally, families gather on a particular weekend during the year. For instance, my husband's family holds a reunion the last Friday and Saturday of June; whereas my husband's mother's family always gathers the first Sunday of August.

Older members of the family share stories of bygone days, some humorous and some sad, but all of them revealing a glimpse of their lives. It's been said that when an older person dies, it's like a small library burns to the ground. Three weeks after one family reunion, we attended the funeral of an 84-year-old aunt.

That's why I believe it's important to record these memories, either on video, tape recording, pen and paper or even all three – in order to capture the person's mannerisms, voice, and life experiences. Most of the memories are lost forever, unless the next generation passes them on to their children.

"If you don't know where you've been, you don't know where you are going." This old saying, as well as the birth of my daughter, motivated me to record family history, so she would know something about those who came before her.

I've learned that my ancestors were Irish, Scottish, English and German. Considering my five-foot height, I was surprised to find out my great-grandfather on my father's side was quite tall. But I figure I inherited my petite size from my mother and her mother and her mother – all of them short women.

It's been said that the faintest ink is better than the strongest memory, so I began writing family history in a notebook. Then, I made copies for brothers, sisters, first cousins, aunts, uncles, and other kinfolk.

What I treasure most is knowing my heritage of faith. My mother's father established two churches and pastored another one for 16 years. Being the eldest grandchild, I'm old enough to remember hearing my grandparents pray together.

The Bible records quite a bit of information concerning family history. Though not the most inspiring portions of Scripture, one can read several chapters of lineages listing who begat whom. These names are important in the life of Jesus, proving his mother's ancestry and fulfilling centuries-old prophecies about Him.

Then there's the aging Apostle Paul who wrote to a young man named Timothy, reminding him of the genuine faith "which dwelt first in your grandmother Lois and your mother Eunice" (2 Timothy 1:5 NKJ).

My husband's grandmother, who saw "two years before the turn of the century," (as she would say), wrote her life story not too many years before she passed away. She told about picking cotton, riding to church in a wagon, and carrying water from the spring to wash clothes. Though times were often hard raising 11 children, she thanked God for her family and left her descendants these words, "God has blessed us in so many ways.... He promised never to leave us alone. How I do love Him." These are precious memories that challenge our generation.

REMEMBERING MY PARENTS' PRAYER FOR DIVINE PROVISION

My parents were married on August 9, 1953 and celebrated 59 years together before my dad passed away several years ago. Being the eldest of their three children, I remember most of those years.

However, one of their life experiences happened when they were young newly-weds. Every time I've heard the story, it reminds me of a powerful principle. When we ask God to meet our needs, He will answer. How and when is up to Him, and sometimes it's amazing.

In January 1955, my dad graduated from a Bible college in Lakeland, FL. He then accepted a call to pastor a small, struggling church in Kingstree, S.C. The congregation's membership matched the income they gave their minister – both were sparse. My parents set up housekeeping in a little, white frame house next door to the church.

During the move, my mother found out she was pregnant. The next few months at the new pastorate proved their faith. Sundays, the offerings were mostly off. Church bills were paid first, then the treasurer paid my dad whatever was left over.

About a month before I was born, they experienced one of their most trying times. Although my mother and father were anxiously looking forward to becoming new parents, the last month of my mom's pregnancy proved to be the leanest month financially.

Their shoestring lifestyle grew shorter and tighter, even for the essentials. They watched their cupboard gradually going bare. The young couple considered calling their parents for assistance, but decided to trust God a few more days.

One of those mornings, my parents awoke to eat the only remaining food in the house. For breakfast, they toasted the last two slices of bread. My dad poured the last glass of milk for my mom and he drank water. Lunch looked unlikely.

As noon approached, my parents exercised their faith by setting the table. Then they pulled out their chairs and sat down in front of their empty plates. While saying grace, my parents made their necessary and urgent request to God.

The two of them sat at the table, glancing at the clock and their reflections in the plates. A half hour passed before my parents heard a knock at their back door. One of their neighbors, a man who did not attend the church, was standing there. He began to tell them that a hired cook had mistakenly prepared lunch, forgetting that his family was about to leave town for a week.

The neighbor asked if they would eat the meal, so the food would not be wasted. In a few minutes, the cook was carrying a pot roast and vegetables into the kitchen. Since the neighbor was going to be away, he asked if they would gather all the ripe harvest in his garden while he was gone.

Whenever my faith wavers, I remember the promise in Philippians 4:19 that "God shall supply all (my) needs according to His riches in glory by Christ Jesus." And I recall how God answered my parents' prayer and supplied divine provision for them and for me – before I was born. And, my faith is strengthened.

WHERE IS YOUR HEART?

Someone once told me a humorous story about a Sunday School teacher and a little boy in her class. It seems she was teaching children about asking Jesus to come into their hearts.

To help them understand the theological principle, she began by asking the youngsters, "Can anyone tell me where your heart is?" A little fellow stood up and patted the seat of his pants and said, "My heart is right here."

His unexpected answer caused the teacher to ask him how he knew his heart was there. He replied, "When I go to my grandma's house, she puts her arms around me and pats me back there with her hand and says, 'Bless his little heart.'"

Where is your heart, spiritually speaking? Jesus said, "For where your treasure is, there your heart will be also" (Mathew 6:21 NKJ). He wanted you and me to know that what we value most reveals the truth about our hearts – be it money, prestige...you name it.

In the Bible, we find other scriptures that help us examine our hearts and God's remedies for our ills. What does a check-up tell us about our hearts and why is that important? That's how we find out the kind of person we are.

Proverbs 23:7 says as a person "thinks in his heart, so is he" (NKJ). The heart can be "deceitful... and desperately wicked," according to Jeremiah 17:9.

God provides the remedy when we pray, "Create in me a clean heart, O God" (Psalm 51:10 KJV). Jesus has promised, "Blessed are the pure in heart, for they shall see God" (Matthew 5:8 KJV).

Maybe your heart is sick because you have lost hope, as the Bible describes in Proverbs 13:12. But the remedy can be found in Proverbs 17:22 where we read that a merry heart is good medicine. And, God will supply the gladness to make our hearts merry (Psalm 4:7).

"Let not your heart be troubled..." Jesus tells us to believe in Him (John 14:1 KJV). He said He came to heal the broken-hearted.

The Apostle Paul tells us we should, "Be kind one to another, tenderhearted, forgiving one another as God for Christ's sake hath forgiven you" (Ephesians 4:32 KJV). It's amazing to think that through Christ's forgiveness of our sins He lives in our hearts. "For with the heart one believes unto righteousness, and with the mouth confession is made unto salvation" (Romans 10:10 NKJ).

Do you want to be sure Jesus is in your heart? There's a familiar Sunday School song whose words simplify this theological principle. You may want to prayerfully sing them or say them.

"Into my heart, into my heart, come into my heart, Lord Jesus. Come in today, come in to stay. Come into my heart, Lord Jesus."

DO YOUR BATTERIES NEED TO BE RECHARGED?

There's a story told about a missionary in Africa whose car wouldn't crank. So, he came up with an ingenious way to start the car by parking on a hill and getting nearby school children to give the car a push.

For two years, the missionary started his car this way. Then, health problems forced a decision to return to the States. When the new missionary arrived, the older man explained the method for cranking the car.

The new missionary raised the hood and spotted the problem, "You just need to tighten this loose battery cable." The new missionary sat in the driver's seat, turned the ignition and the car cranked immediately because of a better connection.

What would we do without batteries? They operate our cars (hopefully, more so in the future). Batteries power our portable telephones, hearing aids, TV remote control, pacemakers, and more.

Digital cameras quickly drain the power from batteries, so I use rechargeable ones for my camera. I can plug in these batteries and restore them to full strength by leaving them plugged in overnight.

Batteries come in different shapes and sizes.... like people. And, every one of us needs recharging regularly. Our physical strength gets depleted by work and sickness. Worry and stress will zap our energy.

How do people like you and me get "recharged" physically, emotionally, mentally, and spiritually? Here are some remedies I've researched.

Physically, we need to recharge our bodies by eating

right and getting enough sleep each night. Mentally and emotionally, do something for the kid in you. There's medical proof that laughter boosts the immune system by releasing a natural chemical in the brain.

One researcher has found that laughter lowers blood pressure. "Laughing relaxes the body and reduces problems associated with high blood pressure, strokes, arthritis, and ulcers." Laughter truly is good medicine – just like the Bible says (Proverbs 17:22).

Let's look at three ways to recharge spiritually. First, reconnect by rest and quiet time. Jesus took time to come aside and be alone with God. Jesus promises, "Come to Me, all you who labor and are heavy laden, and I will give you rest" (Matthew 11:28 NKJ). Vance Havner once said, "Jesus knows we must come apart and rest a while, or else we may just plain come apart."

Second, reconnect with prayer, even when you don't feel like praying or think you're too busy. Have you ever heard that seven days without prayer makes one w-e-a-k? Draw near to God and He will draw near to you.

Remember this third way to recharge your batteries. Reconnect by Scripture reading. Take time to read your favorite verses - the ones underlined in your Bible. Print a Bible promise on an index card and tape it to your mirror as a reminder of God's Word.

Despite what the cute battery commercial says, people can't "keep going and going and going." Remember that we aren't much use to anyone when we need our "batteries recharged."

HOLOCAUST SURVIVOR FORGAVE CONCENTRATION CAMP GUARD

One of my favorite books, *The Hiding Place*, tells the life story of Corrie Ten Boom and her family who lived in Holland during World War II. Reading about her makes me wish I could have met this courageous lady. One day, we will have eternity to talk.

The book's title describes a secret staircase and room of Corrie's home where her family hid their Jewish neighbors from the Nazis. Before the end of the war, the German soldiers discovered her family's activities and arrested them. They were sent to a concentration camp called Ravensbruck.

Corrie Ten Boom was the only member of her family who returned home after the Holocaust. Due to an error in paperwork, she was mistakenly released from the concentration camp on December 28, 1944. Just a week later, an order was issued to kill all women her age and older.

After the war, Corrie began traveling in Europe and America telling about her experience of survival and sharing a message of God's forgiveness. In her book, she relates an incident that happened while in Ravensbruck.

One day when she and her older sister, Betsie, were forced to stand naked, they saw a concentration camp matron beating another prisoner. "Oh, the poor woman," Corrie cried. "Yes, may God forgive her," Betsie replied. Corrie realized that her sister was once again praying for souls of the brutal Nazi guards.

Years later while Corrie Ten Boom was speaking to a group of people, she recognized a familiar face in the audience. The person approached her at the conclusion of her remarks, and Corrie felt anger growing inside her. The individual had been one of the guards at Ravensbruck. He'd asked God to forgive him for the cruel things he had done there, but he wanted to ask Corrie's forgiveness as well.

"Even as the angry vengeful thoughts boiled through me, I saw the sin of them. Jesus Christ had died for this man; was I going to ask for more? Didn't he and I stand together before an all-seeing God convicted of the same murder? For I had murdered him with my heart and my tongue."

Corrie said, "It could not have been many seconds that he stood there, hand held out, but to me it seemed hours as I wrestled with the most difficult thing I had ever had to do." She remembered Jesus' words, "If you do not forgive men their trespasses, neither will your Father forgive your trespasses" (Matthew 6:15 NKJ).

She then grasped the hand of the former guard, "And as I did, an incredible thing took place. The current started in my shoulder, raced down my arm, sprang into our joined hands. And then this healing warmth seemed to flood my whole being, bringing tears to my eyes."

Among my collection of favorite quotations, several come from Corrie ten Boom's many books. She once wrote, "You never so touch the ocean of God's love as when you forgive and love your enemies." Corrie learned, "When He tells us to love our enemies, He gives, along with the command, the love itself."

MIZ LOU BROWN'S "SHIPS OF LIFE"

I count it a privilege to have known Pat and Lou Brown. Visits with them in the two-story, rambling house down on their farm in southern Covington County were unforgettable.

Getting out of the car, we were always greeted by their guineas screeching, "Packrat," something shocking to a city girl who had never heard those noisy birds. Mr. Pat always made coffee and they both made interesting conversation.

Miz Lou, as she was affectionately called, wrote a column in the Andalusia Star-News for many years. Many years ago, a collection of her columns was published in the book titled, "My Country Roads."

Her wit and wisdom made me want to spend time with Miz Lou and read her words. After several visits with her, I wanted to write her biography. Having interviewed with Miz Lou and Mr. Pat for a newspaper article, I knew her life story would be an inspiration to others. Their courtship story reminds me of the novel, *Christy*, by Katherine Marshall.

When doctors told Miz Lou she had cancer, I determined it was time to approach her with the idea. "What if we get started and I kick the bucket?" she said matter-of-factly. Maybe she didn't consider her life interesting content for a book, or didn't want to spend the last days of her life writing about her years.

During a visit one afternoon, she mentioned a speech she had given to a youth group. She talked to them about the "ships of life." Let me tell you about those ships that we sail on through this voyage we call life. I've added a few more to Miz Lou's list.

Come aboard citizenship. It offers rights and responsibilities like voting and paying taxes. Get involved in your community and you might even find yourself in leadership.

Set your sails on scholarship. Start this trek from the first day of school by earning high marks. Scholarship continues beyond higher education. Learning is a lifelong apprenticeship.

Everyone experiences relationship. Your parents, spouse, and children are important passengers on your travel through life, not to mention people with whom you form lasting friendships. Enjoy the fellowship of spending time with close friends.

The most crucial relationship to establish is a personal relationship with Jesus Christ. It involves more than church membership. Your duty will include discipleship and worship to our Creator. As the Psalmist wrote, "Oh come, let us worship and bow down; Let us kneel before the Lord our Maker" (Psalm 95:6 NKJ).

You will find strength to face the storms of life that bring hardships when you spend time in fellowship with Christ. Take it from a first century writer who traveled by ship to preach the Gospel. The apostle Paul tells us that Christians can find strong encouragement by holding fast to our hope in God. It's a hope, sure and steadfast, that is an anchor for the soul.

PREPARE TO GIVE AN ACCOUNT BEFORE YOUR DEADLINE

"In this world nothing can be said to be certain, except death and taxes," Benjamin Franklin wrote in a letter to a French scientist and close friend in 1789. The often-quoted statement is as true now as then.

Margaret Mitchell's famous character Scarlett O'Hara exclaimed, "Death and taxes and childbirth! There's never any convenient time for any of them." I imagine that when it comes to paying income taxes, some people may feel their money is "gone with the wind."

Now, I'm not an income tax professional, but as a taxpayer I do know tax forms require us to give an account of ourselves. The forms require our name and address. We mark whether we're married or single and list our dependents. We must report our income and expenses.

There's a line to record our occupations, the job where we earn the money on which the tax dollars are due. We tell how much we gave to our church or charitable organizations. In other words, the IRS knows a lot about us from the tax return we file.

Did you know the subject of taxes can be found in the Bible? For instance, Jesus paid taxes. In Matthew chapter 17, the temple tax collectors asked Peter whether or not Jesus was going to pay what amounted to two days wages. Jesus told Peter to go fishing, and the first fish he caught would have a coin in its mouth to pay for His and Peter's taxes.

Jesus could provide for us in the same way if He wanted to. Instead, He gives us the strength for each day to earn a living and pay taxes. So, don't use a poor catch of fish as an excuse for not paying taxes.

In Matthew 22, the Pharisees asked Jesus whether taxes should be paid. Jesus held up a coin and asked what image was imprinted on it. They replied, "Caesar," the ruler of their government. Jesus told them to give Caesar what he is due, and we who are made in the image of God should give God what He is due – ourselves.

Think about the two words – "the IRS." Together, they spell the word – "theirs" because we owe it. We belong to God, who paid a debt we could not pay by sending His Son to die for our sins. We are His, if we ask Him to forgive us. God knows much more about us than the IRS. According to Matthew - a tax collector turned disciple - He even knows the number of hairs on our head, and God also knows our hearts.

After taxes and death, there's something else that is certain. Hebrews 9:27 says all of us will die and after this comes the judgment and "every one of us shall give an account of himself to God" (Romans 14:12 NKJ). Like Scarlett O'Hara said, there's no convenient time for death. Only God knows our last day, so we'd better be prepared for our "deadline."

GOD CAN MAKE A WAY
WHEN THERE SEEMS TO BE NO WAY

Has this ever happened to you? You get out of your car, lock all the doors, and suddenly realize you've left your key inside the car.

Someone has said that confession is good for the soul. I've locked my key in my car more times than I care to admit. Sometimes having too many things on my mind distracts me momentarily when I step out of the car. Other times, I'm just plain forgetful.

Like me, maybe you know all too well the frantic feeling of searching for a car key only to realize it's still in the ignition or on the front seat. It seems even more discouraging when all the windows are rolled up tightly.

A friend once gave me some wise words of advice she learned from someone after such an avoidable incident had occurred. Keep your keys in your hand until you get out of the vehicle, and use them to lock the door. Then put them in your purse or pocket. Or else buy one of those hide-a-key magnets and always keep a spare key in it.

My personal experiences came to mind when I read about a man who was sitting in his parked car on a street. A young woman, whose car was in the next parking space, approached him and asked if he had a hammer.

When he said no, she went to speak with the man in the car in front of hers. He handed her a hammer that he found in his toolbox. Then, she walked back to her car and proceeded to smash the vent window on the driver's side of her car. Upon returning the hammer, she opened her door, took out the keys, and waved to them with a triumphant grin.

As she drove away, the fellow who loaned the woman a hammer spoke to the man still sitting in his car. "If only she had told me why she wanted the hammer, I could have helped her. I'm a locksmith," he said.

The minister went on to compare the way we live with the actions of the woman. We hammer away at the fragile and valuable things we don't understand and cannot solve, when there is power available to us for the asking.

A hymn writer penned these familiar words, "Oh, what peace we often forfeit. Oh, what needless pain we bear. All because we do not carry everything to God in prayer." Remember, if it matters to you, it matters to God.

Jesus promises, "Ask, and it shall be given you; seek, and ye shall find; knock, and it shall be opened unto you" (Matthew 7:7 KJV).

There are times when unforeseen things happen or we get into situations of our own making and we can do little, if anything, about it. We must admit we need help and wait for it to come. God can make a way when there seems to be no way, if we'll ask Him.

A SPECIAL PRAYER FOR ANY SITUATION

Though no one knows for sure who wrote this special prayer, it's often attributed to Reinhold Niebuhr, who included the words in a sermon he preached in 1943 during World War II.

Most people have never heard of the Protestant theologian, but most of us have read his familiar words. The name of the prayer comes from the first line, written when the world was in desperate need of peace and serenity. The words were published in a book of prayers for military chaplain. Here's the original version.

"God, give us the grace to accept with serenity the things that cannot be changed, Courage to change the things which should be changed, and the Wisdom to distinguish the one from the other."

The Serenity Prayer actually has eleven more lines. The words make the prayer even more meaningful for any situation we face in life.

"Living one day at a time, Enjoying one moment at a time, Accepting hardship as a pathway to peace, taking, as Jesus did, This sinful world as it is, not as I would have it, Trusting that You will make all things right, If I surrender to Your will."

Though Niebuhr's words were written as a prayer, they give us practical principles to live by when facing life's challenges and decisions. Every day is a gift from God.

Someone once said we can wake up and face the new day one of two ways - "Good morning, Lord," or "Good Lord, it's morning!"

We need to ask Him for His grace, His courage and His wisdom. The Lord promises us in His Word that His grace is sufficient for His strength is made perfect in our weakness (2 Corinthians 12:9 KJV).

Pastor and author Chuck Swindoll once said, "Wisdom is the God-given ability to see life with rare objectivity and to handle life with rare stability." The Bible tells us if anyone lacks wisdom, "let him (or her) ask of God…and it shall be given him" (James 1:5 KJV).

No one gets out of life alive. Ailments, accidents or old age will cause us one day to breathe our last breath. George Bernard Shaw remarked, "The statistics on death are quite impressive – one out of one people die."

How can hardship, suffering and eventually death be the pathway to peace? Christians learn to trust in God no matter what the situation and find peace that passes all understanding.

PGA tour player Paul Azinger wrote a book about his battle with cancer. When Paul was undergoing chemotherapy and didn't know if he was going to live or die, he experienced joy and peace. Fellow golfer Payne Stewart asked him, "How can you have that kind of peace?" Azinger replied with a quote he had heard, "We aren't in the land of the living going to the land of the dying. We're in the land of the dying, going to the land of the living."

God has a plan and purpose for each of us to fulfill during our lifetimes, if we will surrender to His will.

UNDERSTANDING THE LANGUAGE OF TEARS

Tears, those salty drops of liquid that spill from your eyes, speak a language of their own. They are the ink of the soul revealing our emotions. Tears flow like splashes of joy when a good laugh squeezes them from the corners of your eyes.

In times of loss, tears can flood from your eyes in seemingly endless streams down your cheeks. French philosopher Voltaire has written, "Tears are the silent language of grief."

Feelings, like embarrassment, excitement, anger or anxiety can cause someone to burst into tears. Another writer put it this way, "Tears are the safety valve of the heart when too much pressure is laid on it."

Physically, tears express the pain we feel - whether a spontaneous "ouch" or unspeakable agony. Herbert Lockyer has said, "Tears are liquid pain." They know no age limit. A newborn announces its arrival by crying. In a nursing home we once visited, an Alzheimer's patient walked the halls sobbing.

Tears have a way of making their appearance at family events such as weddings and funerals. My husband's aunt, whose eyes welled up with tears every time she told a family memory, once said, "My heart is too close to my eyes."

This warm fluid from glands around the eyeball fights bacteria and keeps dust out of the eyes. Every time we blink, tears bathe the outer layer of the eye, called the cornea. Without tears, dryness would result in blindness. Recently, I experienced a dryness that required eye drops.

Max Lucado, one of my favorite authors, wrote a book years ago entitled *No Wonder They Call Him The Savior*, which ranks as one of the best books I've ever read. In one chapter called "Miniature Messengers," Lucado writes, "When words are most empty, tears are most apt."

The author paints a vivid word picture of the people and events surrounding Christ's death. He describes the tear-stained faces at the foot of the cross, like that of John, the disciple whom Jesus asked to take care of His weeping mother.

Then there's Peter, the fisherman turned disciple, who spent three years with Christ then denied knowing Him after He was arrested. Later, Peter wept bitterly (Matthew 26:75).

Did you know that the shortest verse in the Bible has only two words, "Jesus wept" (John 11:35)? Jesus shed tears when taken to the grave of His friend, Lazarus, and then Jesus raised him from the dead.

As Jesus drew near Jerusalem for His triumphal entry, He wept over the city saying, "How I wish today that you of all people would understand the way to peace. But now it is too late" (Luke 19:42 New Living Translation). Sometimes I wonder if we shouldn't weep for the soul of America.

Max Lucado has written, "When tears come, remember Jesus. Remember, the eyes of God wept human tears."

RUTH GRAHAM'S LIFETIME UNDER CONSTRUCTION

Many years ago, Ruth Bell Graham, wife of Evangelist Billy Graham, wrote about a sign she had seen on a highway whose words she would like to have on her tombstone.

It read, "End of construction. Thank you for your patience." Reading about Ruth's life after she died, I came across her humorous, yet thought-provoking comment. The words are, in fact, on her tombstone. Ruth's lifetime "construction project" lasted 87 years. Born in China to missionary parents, this wife, mother, and author was known as a woman of prayer.

President Bush described her as, "A remarkable woman of faith whose life was defined by her belief in a personal, loving, and gracious God. She was an encouraging friend, accomplished poet, and devoted mother of five and grandmother of 19."

Ruth's daughter, Anne Graham Lotz, shared some of her mother's words of advice. Anne quoted one of her sayings, "Make the most of all that comes, and the least of all that goes." She remarked, "My Mother was in love with Jesus…and that love was contagious. She taught me by her example that Jesus is everything."

A Sunday School song I learned several years ago comes to mind when I look back on my life. "He's still working on me to make me what I ought to be. It took Him just a week to make the moon and stars, the sun and the earth, and Jupiter and Mars. How loving and patient He must be. He's still working on me."

God has a blueprint for your life and mine. His plan can be found by reading His Word and seeking His guidance in

WHAT ARE PEOPLE READING WHEN THEY SEE YOU?

Bumper stickers are a commentary on our culture today. Some proudly announce a child's honor roll achievement in school. Others declare their loyalty to a college or high school team, easily recognized by the Tiger, Elephant, Bulldog, or Bobcat, Eagle or school colors printed on it.

Though they can come in all shapes and sizes, most bumper stickers are rectangular with enough space for a few words. They deliver a message the driver wants others to see.

"American by birth, Southern by the grace of God" speaks of pride in one's heritage. "Vehicle Insured by Smith and Wesson" warns a potential thief of the owner's gun. A humorous phrase based on a Disney movie says, "I owe, I owe, so off to work I go."

People campaign for their candidate with a bumper sticker or stand up for an issue. In recent years, with our country at war, many folks have placed American flags and patriotic quotes like "God bless the USA" on their cars, trucks, and vans. Other messages remind us to "Pray for our troops" or "Support our soldiers."

Whatever a bumper sticker says, whoever travels behind a vehicle with one or more cannot help but read it, especially at an intersection while the light is red. That's why, for me, it's sometimes revolting to follow a car with curse words or downright vulgar statements.

Bumper stickers can carry a witness for Christ. Some of these ask, "Have you prayed about it?" or "Got Jesus?" or comments like "God forgives. Let Him."

A series of billboards and bumper stickers a few years

ago were designed as messages from God. "Does the road you're traveling lead to My house?" and "That love thy neighbor thing – I meant it."

Familiar sayings were once quite popular on bumper stickers such as "WWJD – What Would Jesus Do?" or "Christians aren't perfect, just forgiven."

Sadly, on more than one occasion, I've read the following words on a vehicle in front of me. "Heaven doesn't want me and Hell's afraid I'll take over." This bumper sticker speaks volumes about the owner of that vehicle, but that person couldn't be more wrong.

Heaven does want them. If I could talk to them face to face, I'd tell them that God loves them so much that He gave His only Son to die for their sins. Through Jesus' sacrifice, there is forgiveness and eternal life in heaven God is preparing for those who love and accept Christ as their personal Savior.

Think again about taking over hell. The Bible describes hell as a place of eternal torment and suffering with weeping and wailing. Hell was prepared for the devil. Though human beings are capable of committing unspeakable evil, the devil is the ultimate wicked one.

According to the apostle Paul, Christians, by their lives, are living letters "known and read of all men" (2 Corinthians 3:2 KJV). As someone once said, you and I may be the only Bible a person reads. What are people reading when they see us?

WHAT ARE YOU WAITING FOR?

Time seems to stand still when the red light turns green and the person in front of you doesn't realize it. Who wants to wait when you've got places to go and things to do?

Having to wait in traffic can teach us patience. No one likes to wait, but waiting is a fact of life. Make an appointment to see your doctor and where do you sit until your name is called? The waiting room.

Do you have "call waiting" on your phone? It can be frustrating when the beeps interrupt your conversation. One of my relatives would rather hang up and let me call her back than for me to put her on hold to take an incoming call.

The farmer plants his seed and must wait for the harvest. A high school education requires twelve years of schooling. Like all mothers know, there's a nine month wait before we hold a newborn in our arms. (I waited nine months and two weeks to hold my daughter!)

Waiting is most difficult when you are standing by the bedside of a loved one waiting to see what's going to happen to them.

In *The Path of Waiting*, Henri Nouwen writes, "The secret of waiting is the faith that the seed has been planted and something has begun." Nouwen goes on to say that most people think waiting is a waste of time, but waiting is an act of obedience. It requires a trusting heart. "It is giving up control over our future and letting God define our life."

A Jewish writer, Simone Weil, has said, "Waiting patiently in expectation is the foundation for spiritual life." Sometimes it's hard for me to understand why God doesn't answer my prayers on my time table. That's when I must tell the Lord, "And now, Lord, what do I wait for? My hope is in You" (Psalm 39:7 NKJ).

I'm thankful for promises in the Bible – like Isaiah 40:31 – that say, "They that wait upon the Lord shall renew their strength; they shall mount up with wings as eagles; they shall run, and not be weary, and they shall walk and not faint" (Isaiah 40:31 KJV).

According to quadriplegic artist Joni Erickson Tada, "The times we find ourselves having to wait on others may be the perfect opportunities to train ourselves to wait on the Lord."

Charles Stanley has said, "When we surrender to His timing, He does mighty things in and for us, according to His will and His timing. God acts on behalf of those who wait for Him."

What are you waiting for? Is it a bank loan to buy a house? A job interview? I know several people waiting to hear the doctor's diagnosis. Their future is unknown and uncertain. All they can do is wait.

Often, all we can do is trust God and wait. The Bible says, "Wait on the Lord; Be of good courage, And He shall strengthen (your) heart; Wait, I say, on the Lord!" (Psalm 27:14 KJV)

GOD BLESS AMERICA
IN SONG AND PRAYER

The family of Israel Baline came from Russia and settled in New York in 1893 when Israel was five-years-old. He was one of eight children born to Moses and Leah Baline. His father, a rabbi, died soon after the boy turned 13.

Having only two years of formal schooling, Israel looked for various jobs to help his family survive. He sold newspapers and worked as a street musician. In 1907, Baline wrote the first of more than a thousand songs he would compose during his century of life.

In 1918, Baline was drafted into the Army, a few months after becoming a U.S. citizen. One of his best-known compositions was written while he served in the military, but was not published until 1937. It immediately became a popular patriotic song. We know Israel Baline as Irving Berlin. A misprint on published sheet music changed the spelling of his name.

This Jewish immigrant's song, "God Bless America," has been called our country's unofficial national anthem. Singer Kate Smith introduced it on a radio broadcast on Armistice Day (now called Veterans Day) 1938. Since the terrorist attacks of 9/11, the song has often been sung at ballparks, stadiums, and other public events.

The lyrics composed by this self-taught musician could be described as a prayer, "God bless America, land that I love. Stand beside her and guide her through the night with a light from above."

There's no doubt, when one considers the meaning of the verb bless, that God has truly blessed America during the years since the birth of our nation. The dictionary lists several definitions, one of which is "to make prosperous." No other country in the world has been blessed like America.

This nation that we love is wealthy compared to the rest of the world. We have more food than we can eat and send tons of it to other peoples who are starving. Our poorest citizens are rich compared to those in most countries.

Another definition for bless is "to ask for divine favor." The Bible promises, "Blessed is the nation whose God is the Lord" (Psalm 33:12 KJV). Our country has drifted from Godly principles, as evidenced by our moral decay. But we can turn things around, if God's people will "humble themselves, and pray, and seek His face and turn from their wicked ways," God will hear from heaven and will forgive our sin and heal our land" (2 Chronicles 7:14).

The song goes on to describe the geography of our beautiful homeland that God created, "From the mountains to the prairies, to the ocean white with foam, God bless America, my home sweet home."

Berlin wrote "God bless America" as a prayer for peace prior to World War II. The only verse says, "While the storm clouds gather far across the sea, Let us swear allegiance to a land that's free. Let us all be grateful for a land so fair, As we raise our voices in a solemn prayer." Let's pray daily that God will continue to bless America…our home sweet home.

DOUBTS ABOUT GOD?
TRUST HIS HEART!

Several people I know are battling cancer and cancer seems to be winning - at least for now.

Watching them fight this disease as it attacks various areas of their bodies makes me feel helpless. All I know to do is to continue to pray for them because, like me, they believe in the power of prayer.

But sometimes I wonder if, while they are suffering, maybe in the wee hours of the morning when pain shouts so loud, they may question God about why this is happening to them. But suffering is not the only thing that can cause Christians to doubt God's action.

Talk to anyone who knows God through a personal relationship with His Son, Jesus Christ and they can tell you about times when God seems distant. At times, I feel like my prayers do not rise above the ceiling.

I've read about a book containing a collection of Mother Teresa's personal letters. She never intended for her letters to be published. In fact, she had asked that they be destroyed after her death. Her letters reveal her spiritual struggle through her years in India. In one letter, she'd written, "I came to India with the desire to love Jesus as he has never been loved before." Mother Teresa - described as a simple, pious woman - worked many years in the slums of Calcutta helping the poorest of the poor. But even she experienced times when God seemed far away.

"It's one thing to feel that God is not with you. It's another thing to believe that God doesn't exist," Rev. James Martin, a Jesuit priest and author, says of Mother Teresa. He stresses that her belief in God never wavered.

"Doubt is natural within faith. It comes because of our human weakness and frailty," states theologian Alister McGrath, "Unbelief is the decision to live your life as if there is no God. It is a deliberate decision to reject Jesus Christ and all that he stands for. But doubt is something quite different. Doubt arises within the context of faith. It is a wistful longing to be sure of the things in which we trust."

Henry Drummond, a Scottish author and evangelist, once said, "Christ never failed to distinguish between doubt and unbelief. Doubt is can't believe; unbelief is won't believe. Doubt is honesty; unbelief is obstinacy. Doubt is looking for light; unbelief is content with darkness."

Thomas, one of Jesus' disciples, earned the nickname "Doubting Thomas," because he doubted Jesus' resurrection since he wasn't in the room when Jesus appeared to the disciples for the first time. But eight days later, Thomas was with the disciples in a room (with the doors shut) when Jesus appeared again, and said, "Peace be unto you" (John 20:26 KJV).

Jude 22 says, "Be merciful to those who doubt" (NIV). There's a song that suggests how to trust God when circumstances suggest doubt, "When you don't understand. When you can't see His plan. When you can't trace His hand, trust His heart."

"YOU'VE GOT MAIL," AND IT'S FROM GOD

"You've got mail." Sounds like a greeting from your postman.

"Neither snow, nor rain, nor gloom of night stays these couriers from their swift completion of their appointed rounds," says the familiar motto attributed to the postal service mail carriers who deliver mail six days a week to your personal address. Looks like that may change in the near future to five days a week.

In the age of technology, "you've got mail" is identified with an electronic voice telling you to check your e-mail box. Our ancestors could not imagine sending a message instantly to anyone anywhere in the world who has access to a computer and internet, or a smart phone.

According to recent statistics, there are around four billion email addresses. It's estimated over 300 billion emails are sent every day and 70% of those emails are considered spam – electronic junk mail.

The speed of e-mail as compared to the postal service's regular delivery has caused the latter to earn the nickname "snail-mail." But even the post office can guarantee mail will travel overnight and arrive the next day.

Have you ever heard of V-mail? During World War II, V-mail or Victory mail was the name for the letters exchanged between home and the soldiers fighting in Europe.

Then there's voice mail, the message you leave on answering machines or phone systems as soon as you hear the sound of the tone. While driving around town recently, I noticed a church sign that read, "God answers knee-mail."

I thought, "What a great way to remind people to pray."

Maybe it's the kid in me, but I still look forward to finding a letter in the mailbox addressed to me. A sealed envelope begs to be opened, whether or not the return address is familiar.

You've got mail from God and so do I. "The Bible is a letter God has sent to us," according to theologian Matthew Henry. A patriarch of the faith once said, "Be astounded that God should have written to us."

It's a personal letter written to each one of us that begs to be opened. God's letter tells you and me how much He loves us. The Word of God contains pages of precious promises to us. We can read the epistles or letters that the Apostle Paul wrote from prison to the church members in Corinth, Greece and other places like Ephesus and Galatia. Then there are rules to live by, like the Ten Commandments and Beatitudes.

God's letter is His inspired and infallible Word. Read your Bible like you would your e-mail or letters every day. You can read seemingly numerous translations of the Bible on websites such as www.biblegateway.com. The Bible was "written, that you may believe that Jesus is the Christ, the Son of God; and that believing you may have life in his name" (John 20:31 NIV).

GETTING A GRIP ON
THE CHRISTIAN LIFE

Talk to a new Christian or an older one, who has been serving the Lord for many years, and they'll probably agree that living the Christian life is not easy.

Being a Christian is more than an instantaneous conversion. It's a daily journey of learning to live more and more Christ-like. We must continually deny our old human nature and be transformed by His Spirit into a new nature that intentionally chooses to follow Christ.

Author Charles Swindoll has written, "To be like Christ. That is our goal, plain and simple. It sounds like a peaceful, relaxing, easy objective." He goes on to say, "It is neither easy nor quick nor natural...only Christ can accomplish it within us."

I remember hearing Bible teacher Ian Thomas explain how to live the Christian life. His illustration gives a vivid description of what the Scripture means about Christ living in us.

As a glove is made in the likeness of a hand to contain the hand, so mankind was created in the image of God. There's an emptiness within each of us that can only be filled by a personal relationship with God Himself. We cannot live the Christian life in our own strength and abilities, just as the glove can do nothing without the strength of the hand.

Suppose you told a glove to pick up a book. It's got a thumb and fingers, the shape and form of a hand; but no matter what you tell it to do it's unable to pick up a book. But, as soon as you put your hand into that glove, the glove becomes as strong as your hand. Everything possible with my hand is possible for that glove.

Ian Thomas writes, "You are the glove, Christ is the hand!" The Apostle Paul put it this way, "I can do all things through Christ who strengthens me" (Philippians 4:13 NKJ).

The story is told that Martin Luther, leader of the Reformation during the 1500's, answered a knock at his door. "Does Dr. Luther live here?" the man asked. "No," Luther answered, "he died, Christ lives here now."

The Apostle Paul's testimony should be the testimony of every Christian. He said, "I am crucified with Christ: nevertheless, I live; yet not I, but Christ liveth in me: and the life which I now live in the flesh I live by the faith of the Son of God, who loved me, and gave Himself for me" (Galatians 2:20 KJV).

Pastor and author A.W. Tozer described a real Christian this way. "He feels supreme love for One whom he has never seen, talks familiarly every day to Someone he cannot see, expects to go to heaven on the virtue of Another, empties himself in order to be full, admits he is wrong so he can be declared right, is strongest when he is weakest, richest when he is poorest, and happiest when he feels worst. He dies so he can live, forsakes in order to have, gives away so he can keep, sees the invisible and hears the inaudible."

HUSBAND AND WIFE LIVED A LIFE OF AMAZING LOVE AND GRACE

John met Mary when they were children. In fact, their mothers were best friends.

When their children were very young, the two mothers wondered if John and Mary would someday marry each other. Sadly, John's mother passed away when he was seven.

The two families, the Catlett's and the Newton's, drifted apart when John's father remarried. John followed his father, a captain of a ship, into a life on the sea, as a young teen.

Years later, when John was seventeen, he went to see the Catlett's again. As soon as he laid eyes on fourteen-year-old Mary, he fell in love with her.

However, John had to admit to himself he was totally unworthy of her. He had lived such an immoral and rebellious life even his fellow sailors were shocked by his conduct and coarse language.

Though his mother had taught him the Scriptures and prayed he would become a minister, he rejected the Christian truths he once learned. But he never forgot them.

On the eleventh day of a fierce storm in the North Atlantic, everyone aboard his ship kept pumping water to stay afloat. Survival looked hopeless. John was attempting to steer the ship, trying to hold it on course.

His thoughts turned to Christ and he cried out, "Lord, have mercy on us!" Later, he wrote in his journal about a verse he read that assured him God might still listen to a person beyond saving like him. "If ye then, being evil, know how to give good gifts unto your children: how much more shall your heavenly Father give the Holy Spirit to them that ask him" (Luke 11:13 KJV).

The wretched man was saved and began seeking the Lord in prayer and in the reading of the Scriptures. Mary saw the change in her childhood friend, and the two were married and spent the next forty years together. He wrote that their love "equaled all that the writers of romance have imagined."

John gave up his cruel business in the slave trade about age 30 to work in an office job and then became a minister at age 39. For forty-six years, he preached the Gospel. Much of his ministry was spent in London where he influenced members of Parliament to abolish slavery.

Today, we can read a two-volume collection of John's letters to Mary. He told her, "I am led to think of the goodness of God, who has made you mine, and given me a heart to value you. Thus my love to you, and my gratitude to him, cannot be separated...All other love that is not connected with a dependence on God, must be precarious."

John Newton never ceased to be amazed at God's work in his life. He began writing hymns for Sunday night services at his church. We still sing his words, "Amazing grace how sweet the sound, that saved a wretch like me, I once was lost but now am found, Was blind but now I see."

DON'T GIVE UP!
MOSES WAS ONCE A BASKET CASE TOO!

A friend emailed a picture of a church sign that read, "Don't give up! Moses was once a basket case too!"

I chuckled, but then thought of little baby Moses lying in the basket his mother made for him before she placed him in Egypt's Nile River. She did it to save his life because Pharaoh had issued an order that Hebrew baby boys be killed.

The book of Exodus tells us that Pharaoh's daughter, along with her servants, came to bathe in the Nile and found Moses floating in the water. Or as one person has described it, she came to the "bank" of the Nile and drew out a little "prophet." God used a basket case to become the leader of his nation.

Moses was not the only basket case in the Bible. In the book of Acts, we read that the Apostle Paul found himself in a basket. Not long after his encounter with Christ on the road to Damascus, Paul was preaching that Jesus is the Son of God in the synagogues of that city. Some of the people conspired to silence Paul.

Day and night, they kept watch on the city gates in order to kill him. One night, Paul's friends lowered him in a basket through an opening in the wall to save his life. God rescued Paul - He obviously didn't mind climbing into a basket.

Then, there was the boy with five barley loaves and two small fish who gave his lunch – that his mother probably prepared - to the disciple Andrew, who took it to Jesus. After giving thanks for the food and breaking the bread, Jesus served over 5000 men plus women and children, who ate until they were full. He asked the disciples to gather the leftovers and they filled twelve large baskets with bread.

We say the term "basket case" as slang for "a person who is helpless or incapable of functioning normally, especially due to overwhelming stress, or anxiety," according to Dictionary.com. If the truth be told, most of us have felt like a basket case on more than one occasion, especially during this global pandemic of COVID-19.

Moses still felt like a basket case when God spoke to him at the burning bush in the desert. God told Moses to go to Pharaoh and say, "Let my people go." But Moses made excuses, pointing out his speech impediment. So, God sent Moses' brother, Aaron, to be the spokesman.

God has a purpose and plan for every one of us and He promises, "My grace is sufficient for you," because My strength works best in your weakness (2 Corinthians 12:9 NKJ).

Hudson Taylor, a British missionary to China, once said, "All of God's great men have been weak men who did great things for God because they reckoned on His being with them; they counted on His faithfulness." Like the Apostle Paul, being a basket case may save your life. Be willing, like the boy, to do what you can where you are with what you've got and watch God bless others."

CROSS OF CHRIST
A BRIDGE TO PEACE

There's a story told about two brothers who lived on adjoining farms. One day the brothers had a falling out after 40 years of farming side by side.

They'd shared machinery and traded goods as needed without a hitch until a small misunderstanding grew into a major difference. Finally, it exploded into an exchange of bitter words, followed by weeks of silence.

One morning, there was a knock at the door of the older brother named John. When he opened it, there stood a man with a carpenter's toolbox. "I'm looking for a few days' work," he said. "Perhaps you would have a few small jobs here and there I could help you with?"

"Yes," said John. "I do have a job for you. Look across the creek at that farm," he pointed toward the water. "That's my neighbor. In fact, it's my younger brother.

"A few weeks ago, there was a meadow between us. He took his bulldozer to the river levee and now there is a creek between us. Well, he may have done this to spite me, but I'll go him one better." John showed the carpenter a pile of lumber by his barn. "I want you to build me a fence, an eight-foot fence, so I won't need to see his place or his face anymore."

The carpenter paused and said, "I think I understand the situation. Give me the nails and a post-hole digger and I'll be able to do a job that will please you." After helping the carpenter get all the things he needed, John had to go to town most of the day. The carpenter worked hard all day - measuring, sawing, and nailing.

The farmer returned about sunset, just as the carpenter

finished his job. John's jaw dropped when he saw what the carpenter had built. Instead of a fence, there was a bridge stretching from one side of the creek to the other.

And, the younger brother was coming across the bridge with his hand outstretched, "You are quite a fellow to build this bridge after all I've said and done." The two brothers met in the middle, shook hands and started talking.

About that time, they turned to see the carpenter standing nearby, lifting his toolbox on his shoulder. The older brother hollered, "Wait. Stay a few days. I've a lot of other projects for you to do."

The carpenter replied, "I'd love to stay awhile, but I have many more bridges to build." George Herbert once wrote, "He that cannot forgive others, breaks the bridge over which he himself must pass if he were to reach heaven; for everyone has need to be forgiven."

A Jewish carpenter, born over 2000 years ago, came to build a bridge between mankind and God. The Bible says, "All have sinned," (Romans 3:23 KJV) and our sin separates us from a Holy God.

But God loved us so much He sent His Son, Jesus Christ, to the cross to build a bridge reconciling each of us to Him. Through Christ's sacrifice, we can have peace with God.

BLOOM WHERE YOU ARE PLANTED

A remarkable event occurs in our yard in the early spring each year. The redbud tree, with its purple blooms, signals the arrival of Spring. Tiny blossoms begin to appear on its bare branches.

Our family has always looked forward to the few weeks the beautiful redbud tree displays its flowering branches. After Easter, the small blossoms form a colorful carpet beneath the tree and green leaves will replace the flowers until Fall.

To understand what makes this event remarkable, you have to know what happened to this tree over twenty years ago. The day after Hurricane Opal left her mark on our county, we walked outside to find the redbud tree had been blown down into our driveway. It was one of six trees the storm snapped or uprooted.

Due to the damage, we cut through the trunk and hauled away the leafy branches. Only the stump remained, pulled to a ninety-degree angle by the winds until most of the roots were exposed.

To our delight and wonder, the next year we discovered tall, wire-like branches shooting upward from the side of the lifeless-looking stump. On the branches were the tiny flowers that tell us winter is over.

Looking at the new life on the redbud tree every Spring reminds me of the real message of Easter. God's creation seems to be telling His Son's story of death and resurrection.

Jesus once said, "I am the resurrection and the life: he that believes in Me though he were dead, yet shall he live" (John 11:25 KJV). Ministers often refer to this scripture to comfort the family of a deceased loved one who was a

Christian. Those who believe in Christ do have the promise of a reunion in heaven.

But Jesus' words apply to every one of us today. Without a personal relationship with Jesus, you and I are dead as a result of sin; but John 3:16 and Romans 6:23 say believers will receive eternal life.

The redbud tree also reminds me of what it's like to live a Christian life. As the Apostle Paul put it, believers should be rooted in Christ, meaning firm in their faith according to Colossians 2:6 - 7.

You may feel like the storms of life have beaten you down. Circumstances may have seemingly uprooted your faith. No matter what has happened, look upward toward the Son. You'll find a ray of hope that will help you bloom where you're planted.

It might surprise you to know that Albert Einstein said the words, "Bloom where you're planted," to a fellow scientist who was complaining about his low pay and mediocre research assignment. To make his point, Einstein reportedly pointed to a blade of grass that had broken through a slab of concrete.

Someone once said, "An oak tree is an acorn that stood its ground." Look up to the Son, stand tall, and bloom where you're planted.

WHY CHRIST'S WORDS
ARE PRINTED IN RED LETTERS

Ever wonder why there are red letters in the Bible? In the New Testament of most Bibles, you will find the words of Christ printed in red ink.

Before 1900, Bibles were printed entirely in black ink. Today, a few Bibles are printed in black ink for those who prefer it or those who are colorblind and cannot read the color red.

The idea for the red letters in Bibles is attributed to Louis Klopsch, owner and editor of *Christian Herald* Magazine. On June 19, 1899, Klopsch was writing an editorial for the magazine when he read Luke 22:20, "This cup is the new covenant in My blood, which is shed for you" (KJV).

Klopsch realized these were the words of Jesus at the Last Supper when our Lord instituted the observance of Communion. And knowing that blood is red, he asked himself, "Why not a red-letter Bible with red words to be those of Jesus?"

After encouragement from his minister, Klopsch sought the help of eminent Bible scholars from America and Europe to submit passages that should be written in red.

In the November 1901 issue of the *Christian Herald*, a large advertisement offered red letter Bibles to readers. The first printing on his own press numbered 60,000 copies. These quickly sold, and the presses had to run "day and night to supply the demand."

Klopsch wrote, "Modern Christianity is striving zealously to draw nearer to the great Founder of the Faith.... This Red-Letter Bible has been prepared and issued in the full conviction that it will meet the needs of the student, the worker, and the searchers after truth everywhere."

He also believed, "In the Red-Letter Bible, more clearly than in any other edition of the Holy Scriptures, it becomes plain that from beginning to end the central figure upon which all lines of law, history, poetry, and prophecy converge is Jesus Christ, the Savior of the world."

Louis Klopsch received a congratulatory message from the King of Sweden and an invitation from President Theodore Roosevelt to come to the White House, which he accepted. Klopsch died March 28, 1910.

What makes this story interesting is the way Jesus' words stood out to Klopsch. All the Bible is inspired by God (2 Timothy 3:16) and the words in red are equally important as other scripture.

However, Jesus' words help us know Him and His teachings. He taught some profound principles that still apply to us today. For instance, "Whoever wants to save his life will lose it, but whoever loses his life for me will find it" (Matthew 16:25 NIV).

"The Word became flesh and dwelt among us," according to John 1:14 (KJV). I like the way a song writer has described the red words of Christ and His blood shed on the Cross. "I love you, I love you, That's what Calvary says. I love you, I love you, I love you written in red."

GOD CREATED
THE AMAZING HUMAN BODY

I once read some interesting facts about the human body that amazed me.

A human being loses an average of 40 to 100 strands of hair a day. An average human scalp has 100,000 hairs. Beards are the fastest growing hairs on the human body. If the average man never trimmed his beard, it would grow to nearly 30 feet long in his lifetime.

A cough releases an explosive charge of air that moves at speeds up to 60 mph compared to a sneeze that can exceed 100 mph. You blink your eyes about 20,000 times a day. Your heart beats about 100,000 times a day.

Your body contains ten to twelve pints of blood. Each square inch of human skin consists of twenty feet of blood vessels. Placed end to end, all your body's blood vessels would measure 62,000 miles.

The average brain weighs three pounds. There are 10 million nerve cells in your brain. Your brain sends messages at the rate of 240 mph. The small intestines are about 25 feet long; however, the large intestines are three times wider than the small intestines. About 400 gallons of blood flow through your kidneys every day.

Babies are born with 300 bones, but by adulthood we have only 206 in our skeleton. We have 230 joints in our bodies. Children have 20 first teeth and adults have 32 teeth.

After conception in our mothers' wombs, every human spent about half an hour as a single cell. At only nineteen days after life begins, your eyes begin to develop. Eventually, each eye will have six million cones, which help you see color and 120 million rods, which help you see black and white.

Your heart begins to beat at day 22 in the womb. By the sixth week, brain waves are detectable and at eight weeks, every organ is in place and the fetus can begin to hear. Weeks nine and ten, teeth begin to form. A baby can turn its head and it can also hiccup.

An unborn baby 's fingerprints appear at three months, when a mother usually finds out she's pregnant. By months five and six, mothers can feel their baby move. He or she is now twelve inches long or more and weighs up to one and a half pounds.

All of these facts remind me of the words of King David who wrote, "For You formed my inward parts; You covered me in my mother's womb. I will praise You, for I am fearfully and wonderfully made; Marvelous are Your works, and that my soul knows very well. My frame was not hidden from You, when I was made in secret.... Your eyes saw my substance, being yet unformed" (Psalm 139:13-17 NKJ).

Anne Graham Lotz writes, "Where did the Creator begin? Did He start with a skeletal frame?" She adds, "Did He next place the heart that pumps seventy-two times a minute, forty million times a year? Truly, we are fearfully and wonderfully and lovingly and personally created by an awe-inspiring, loving Creator" who started with nothing!

ONE PERSON CAN
MAKE A DIFFERENCE

Never underestimate the impact of one person when it comes to speaking up for Biblical principles. A 4th-century monk from Asia named Telemachus illustrates that impact.

One day, Telemachus felt the Lord was telling him to go to Rome. Though he didn't know why, the monk obeyed and began the long walk westward, arriving during a holiday festival.

Telemachus thought perhaps God had a special purpose for him at this particular time. He followed the crowds into the Coliseum, where gladiator contests were staged, something he had never heard of.

The monk realized the horrible violence that was about to begin when the gladiators shouted to the emperor, "We who are about to die salute thee."

Crowds cheered as men killed each other for amusement. Telemachus jumped to his feet to stop the savagery. "In the name of Christ, forbear!" he cried. No one paid any attention. The monk ran down the stone steps and onto the sandy floor of the arena.

Telemachus came between the muscular gladiators. One hit him with his shield, shoving the monk to the ground. Telemachus picked himself up and ran between the gladiators shouting again, "In the name of Christ, forbear!" He could not be silent.

The crowd began to laugh and cheer on the monk, thinking he was part of the entertainment. Telemachus' actions blocked the view of one of the contestants, who barely missed his opponent's blow. Then the crowd turned against the monk, crying for his blood.

In an instant, a gladiator raised his sword and struck Telemachus, slashing down his chest and into his stomach. The monk gasped and weakly uttered his last words, "In the name of Christ, forbear!"

As the gladiators and the crowd looked at the little man's body on the bloody sand, the arena grew deathly silent. A strange thing happened. Someone on the top row of the Coliseum got up and walked out; followed by another and another until all the spectators left the huge stadium.

History records that was the last day gladiator contests were fought to the death there. Because one man stood up for what was right, men never again killed each other for the crowd's entertainment in the Coliseum.

One person can make a difference. With the issues and problems facing our country, you and I can speak up for Biblical principles. Whatever the cost, determine to make a difference. Who knows but that God may need your voice "for such a time as this" (Esther 4:14 KJV).

Bible teacher Beth Moore has said, "Make no mistake. We are not powerless. We are not too remote and removed to make a difference." Orator Edward Everett Hale made the statement, "I am only one, but I am one. I cannot do everything, but I can do something. And I will not let what I cannot do interfere with what I can do."

LOVE AT FIRST SIGHT
FOR PAT AND LOU BROWN

Some years ago, I visited with an elderly couple and, once again, heard the story of how they met, married and spent the rest of their lives together.

I discovered a cassette on which I'd recorded an interview with this couple 30 years ago. I listened to the voices of Pat and Lou Brown again. My mother-in-law, Marie White, took me to the Brown farm in southern Covington County, AL just before Valentine's Day.

Mr. Pat and Miz Lou celebrated their 57th wedding anniversary in 1982. For the two of them, it was love at first sight. Mis' Lou graduated from Opp High School in 1918 and went on to complete a course of study at Troy Teacher's College in 1920.

She was among three women chosen from hundreds of applicants to teach school in a Cajun community near Mobile under the Southern Baptist Missionary Board. They took turns traveling horseback 11 miles into the nearest town to pick up the mail. One summer day in 1923, Lou rode up to the sawmill town's commissary.

She saw Pat sitting in a rocker reading the *Mobile Register*. "The minute I laid my eyes on him, I knew I would marry that man." Lou recalled telling the other teachers that she didn't know his name, but she declared he was the one she was going to marry. In the spring of 1924, one of the other teachers had a date with a young man who asked his friend, Pat Brown, to come along because Pat had a car.

"When Pat walked in the door, I just purely nearly fainted.... I knew the Lord sent him and in two weeks we were married." She remembered they went to Mobile and a

128

federal judge tied the knot. The couple eventually bought a house and 420 acres where they raised seven children in the Beda / Pleasant Home community in south Alabama.

The day of our visit, I was a newlywed of barely three years compared to the Brown's marriage of 57 years. So, I asked for their advice on the subject. Lou and her "precious darling," or "my Love," as she called him, had experienced the joys and sorrows through years of hard times, hard work and lasting love.

A marriage founded on Bible principles is the secret to a happy life, according to Lou, and communication between a man and wife means "everything." Miz Lou wrote regular newspaper column called "My Country Roads," some of which were published in a book by that title in 1979.

She wrote about hearing husbands being described as the presidents and the wives as the vice presidents. "It's plain that the vice president is two or three button holes lower than the president, especially if the vice president is a conservative and is plain spoken."

Miz Lou added, "I've had to eat crow and beg forgiveness so many times in my married life that it's easy for me to fall on my knees and say, 'forgive me." She mentioned Ephesians 5:22, "Wives, submit yourselves unto your own husbands, as unto the Lord" (KJV).

Her words of wisdom speak timeless truth. I'm grateful for the opportunity to get to know Pat and Lou!

WHERE DO YOU
ANCHOR YOUR SOUL?

Meeting different kinds of people makes life interesting. While attending a weekend Christian retreat some time ago, I overheard a man talking about his experiences at sea.

The man looked like a weathered sailor with his white hair combed straight back, forming a curly wave. His short, white beard put his chin on even keel with the top of his head. Turned out, this older fellow with muscular arms worked as a shrimper in Bayou La Batre, AL.

Ironically, the theme for the retreat was "The Anchor Holds." Seeing a picture of an anchor hanging on the wall, I noticed something unique that I'd never seen before.

In between the ring where the rope is secured and the base where a pair of hooks bend upward was the shape of a cross. So, I took advantage of the opportunity to ask an expert with firsthand experience about it.

The shrimper told me the pointed hooks at the base of the anchor are called flukes and the shorter perpendicular bar near the top is known as the crossbar. I also found out the curved end of the anchor is the crown.

He explained that when the anchor is dropped into the water, the crossbar balances the anchor so it doesn't tip from one side to the other.

Without the crossbar, the anchor would likely be unsteady because one of the flukes might not grab hold of the ocean bottom. The sailor's explanation made me see a spiritual application in the anchor. It's in the cross we find the balance we need for our daily lives, especially when the storms of life threaten to sink us.

Where would we be without the hope of our salvation?

The writer of Hebrews describes our hope as "an anchor of the soul, both sure and steadfast" set before us if we will grasp it and hold on to it (6:19 KJV).

Ruth Jones, a mother of five and the wife of a busy pastor, was reading 2 Timothy 3:1, which tells about the last days when perilous times will come. Reading news reports of World War II casualties, having food rationed, and seeing discouragement everywhere, she wondered how people could continue in times like these.

On a small notepad, using a pencil she pulled from her apron pocket, she wrote the words and melody to a hymn we often sing, "In times like these you need a Savior. In times like these, you need an anchor. Be very sure, be very sure your anchor holds and grips the Solid Rock. This Rock is Jesus, yes, He's the One."

There's a Scottish Proverb that says, "Were it not for hope the heart would break." Someone once wrote, "Hope is faith holding out its hand in the dark." Thomas Brooks put it this way, "Hope can see heaven through the thickest clouds."

Talking to that mariner reminded me of a Gospel song that echoes the scripture about our hope, "The anchor holds, though the ship is battered. The anchor holds, in spite of the storm. I have fallen on my knees, when I face the raging sea. The anchor holds, in spite of the storm."

INVENTIONS THAT
WERE UNIQUELY INSPIRED

It's an invention many of us use every day. I can't imagine what we ever did without them.

They come in all colors from pastels to neons; but most often pale yellow. This little pad of paper can be as small as two postage stamps or the size of a postcard. No matter the size or color, each little pad of paper has an adhesive strip – hence the common name "sticky notes." We know the brand name as Post-it notes.

According to a CNN article, more than 50 billion Post-it notes are sold every year. But, as Paul Harvey would say, here's the rest of the story.

In 1968, a chemist at the 3M company named Spencer Silver invented a new kind of adhesive made of microspheres that, when attached to paper, will easily be removed and re-attached again. The company could see no use for the invention until 12 years later when another 3M employee was uniquely inspired.

Art Fry came up with the idea during Wednesday night choir practice at his church. Fry would bookmark the songs for the week in his hymnbook with pieces of paper. By Sunday morning, most would have fallen out.

The CNN article quotes Fry, 'I thought what I needed is a bookmark that would stick to the page...without damaging" the hymnbook pages. After using the new "sticky notes" to communicate in the company offices, 3M realized the potential for the product – and now, you know the rest of the story.

Recently, I read about another inventor, Gary Starkweather. An engineer who has worked for Apple,

Microsoft, and Xerox, Starkweather invented the laser printer. He gives credit for the success of his invention to the guidance and inspiration of God.

He once said, "I believe that to a great extent, the creativity we possess is because the Creator put it there. God put things (in us) as tool developers and creative individuals and I think it has to please Him when He sees us use those faculties to make something completely new."

Many other inventors and scientists were inspired by God. George Washington Carver asked God to reveal to him the secrets of the universe. God showed him much about the peanut.

Belief.net says, "The secrets Carver discovered led to the invention of hundreds of new (products) including peanut butter, paint, oil, and plywood." Carver attributed all of his inventions to the Creator, "The Lord has guided me…without my Savior, I am nothing."

Another inventor and noted scientist – Isaac Newton – once said, "Gravity explains the motions of the planets, but it cannot explain who set the planets in motion. God governs all things and knows all that is or can be done." As a Christian, we believe that God provides the inspiration, and it is up to us to provide the application.

The Apostle Paul tells us, "And whatever you do in word or deed, do all in the name of the Lord Jesus, giving thanks to God the Father" (Colossians 3:17 NKJ). John Wesley's words come to mind, "Do all the good you can. By all the means you can. In all the ways you can. At all the times you can. To all the people you can. As long as you ever can."

LEARNING HOW TO LIVE
BETWEEN THE STEPS

I once read about a University professor who was invited to speak at a military base. A soldier named Ralph was assigned the task of picking him up at the airport on that December day.

After they had introduced themselves, the two men headed toward the baggage claim. While walking down the concourse, the professor noticed that Ralph kept disappearing in the crowd. First, Ralph helped an older woman whose suitcase had fallen open. The next time Ralph lifted two toddlers up so they could see Santa Claus.

Still again, Ralph detoured to give directions to someone who was obviously lost. The professor recalled how after helping each person Ralph came back with a big smile on his face.

"Where did you learn to do that?" the professor asked the soldier. "Do what?" Ralph replied. "To be so helpful and considerate to others," the professor said. Ralph responded, "During the war, I guess."

Then, the soldier began telling the professor about his tour of duty in Vietnam. It was his job to clear the minefields, and he watched his friends get killed by explosions, one after another.

"I've learned to live between the steps," he said. "I never knew whether the next one would be my last, so I learned to get everything I could out of the moment between when I picked up my foot and when I put it down again. Every step I took was a whole new world, and I guess I've just been that way ever since."

Meeting Ralph was an unforgettable experience for the

professor. Reading about Ralph reminded me that every day is a gift from God - that's why it's called the present.

Helen Keller once said, "Life is either a daring experience or nothing at all." She also declared, "I will not just live my life. I will not just spend my life. I will invest my life." Scottish minister Henry Drummond has written, "You will find as you look back on your life that the moments when you have really lived are the moments when you have done things in the spirit of love."

Jesus said He came, "that (we may) have life, and that (we may) have it more it more abundantly" (John 10:10 KJV). Someone once said, "Abundant life is not determined by how long we live, but how well we live."

There's a Peanuts cartoon by Charles Schulz depicting Lucy talking to Charlie Brown. She begins, "Life is a lot like a deck chair. Some place it to see where they've been. And some so they can see where they are at the present." To which Charlie Brown replies, "I can't even get mine unfolded." Henry David Thoreau observed, "Most men in this world live out their lives in quiet desperation."

In the words of Henry James, "The great use of life is to spend it for something that outlasts it." There's a Gospel song that says, "We have this moment to hold in our hands and to touch as it slips through our fingers like sand; Yesterday's gone and tomorrow may never come, But we have this moment today."

HAVE YOU EVER HEARD
GOD TALKING TO YOU?

One of my favorite authors, Catherine Marshall, wrote a biography about her husband, Senate Chaplain Peter Marshall, after his death.

In *A Man Called Peter*, she tells of an incident that happened to him early in his life. Peter was walking home one dark and starless night from a nearby Scottish village where he worked.

He had difficulty seeing the path as he made his way through the heather-covered fields. Suddenly, he heard a voice say, "Peter!" The urgency in the voice caused him to stand still and he replied, "Yes," trying to focus on who might be speaking through the darkness.

Hearing nothing, he began walking again. Suddenly, he heard the voice again, sounding even more urgent, "Peter!" When he stopped the second time, he stumbled and fell to his knees. Putting out his hand to catch himself, Peter Marshall found there was no ground in front of him.

He felt around in a semicircle and discovered he was on the very brink of an abandoned stone quarry. One more step and he would have plummeted to certain death. The incident made an unforgettable impression on Peter Marshall.

Have you ever heard God talking to you? Some have heard an audible voice, like Peter Marshall. Even though I can't say I've ever heard God speak aloud, He still speaks to me through His inspired Word.

There have been times when I've been reading my Bible and a particular Scripture seemed to leap off the page, helping me understand what was happening in my life.

Other times I've heard His still, small voice speaking silently to my heart – often words of guidance and comfort. At times, I can sense His loving presence as though His arms are wrapped around me.

Psalm 139 tells us there's no place where God is not present. "...where can I flee from your presence? If I go up to the heavens, you are there; if I make my bed in the depths, you are there. If I rise on the wings of the dawn, if I settle on the far side of the sea, even there your hand will guide me, your right hand will hold me fast. If I say, 'Surely the darkness will hide me and the light become night around me,' even the darkness will not be dark to you; the night will shine like the day, for darkness is as light to you" (vs. 7-12 NIV).

Another one of my favorite authors, C.S. Lewis, once said, "We may ignore, but we can nowhere evade the presence of God." The two disciples on the road to Emmaus didn't realize the Risen Lord was walking and talking with them. The Apostle Paul has written that the Lord is "not far from each one of us" (Acts 17:27 NKJ).

People see and hear God every day, they just don't recognize Him. He still speaks to anyone who will listen. When we draw near to God, He promises to draw near to us. Do you hear Him calling out your name?

prayer. Jeremiah 29:11 says, "For I know the plans I have for you," declares the Lord, to give you hope and a future."

It's crucial that we build our lives on the only true foundation – Jesus Christ. We must come together to worship at church, building up each other in the faith.

The story is told of a man who walked by a construction site one day where all kinds of work was going on – dirt moved and cement mixed. The man noticed someone chiseling a stone from a pile at the foot of the new building being constructed.

"What are you trying to do with that rock?" the man asked. The worker pointed to the top of a newly laid stone wall and replied, "I'm shaping it down here, so it'll fit up there."

This story reminds me of one of my favorite verses in the Bible reads, "Being confident of this very thing, that He who has begun a good work in you will complete it until the day of Jesus Christ" (Philippians 1:6 NKJ). God doesn't give up on us, but sometimes we give up on ourselves.

Until our work on earth is completed and we go to heaven, our lives are still under construction. God's not finished with us yet. Is there any area of your life that needs working on today?

PATRIOTIC HYMN
A PICTURE OF AMERICA
AND PRAYER FOR AMERICA

Katharine Lee Bates grew up in Falmouth, Massachusetts. She was the daughter of a Congregationalist minister, who died the month after she was born in 1859.

Her mother, a teacher, made sure her daughter got the best education despite their meager income. Katharine began writing stories when she was nine years old. During her life, she wrote travel books, a textbook on the history of American literature, children's books, and numerous poems.

Following graduation from Wellesley College, she taught five years in public and private high schools before returning to Wellesley where she taught English literature for 40 years.

She was first inspired to write patriotic verse in 1892, when our country marked the 400th anniversary of Columbus' discovery of America.

The next year Katharine accepted a summer teaching position in Colorado. During her travels out west, she visited the World's Columbian Exposition in Chicago, celebrating Columbus' arrival in 1492. To her, the magnificent buildings constructed for this World Fair, many of them white, looked like alabaster – a mineral that's usually a pure white color.

After completing her summer teaching in Colorado, she and some other teachers trekked up to the top of 14,000-foot Pikes Peak. Katharine described the view, penciling it in her notebook, "It was then and there, as I was looking out over the sea-like expanse of fertile country spreading so far under those ample skies, that the opening lines of the hymn floated into my mind."

She penned four verses, each stanza concluding with an earnest prayer. In this hymn and her other writings, Katharine would stress, "We must match the greatness of our country with the goodness of personal godly living." Her statement reminds me of Proverbs 14:34, "Righteousness exalts a nation, but sin is a reproach to any people" (NKJ).

The writer and teacher often spoke of the two stones that played such important roles in our nation's history - the tablets containing the Ten Commandments and Plymouth Rock. She said, "If only we could couple the daring of the Pilgrims with the moral teachings of Moses, we would have something in this country that no one could ever take from us."

The poem Katharine Bates wrote after her trip to Pike's Peak stayed in her notebook for several years until she came across it again in 1899. She sent it to a publisher in Boston. It was first printed in the *Boston Evening Transcript* on November 19, 1904.

After slight revisions in the text over the next 14 years, the poem was set to music composed by Samuel A. Ward, a New Jersey music businessman. The hymn received widespread popularity during the difficult days of World War I. Some suggested that Bates' song should be selected as our national anthem. That poem was "America, the Beautiful."

WHERE DOES THE TIME GO?

Lately, I have found myself somewhat overwhelmed by too much to do and not enough time to do it.

"I've got too much on my plate," I commented to my daughter, who challenged me in her reply, "Who filled your plate?" Somehow, I've managed to crowd too many tasks into my schedule.

Most of us wrestle, from time to time, with the tyranny of the urgent. Often, there is not enough time in the day to get done the things we need or want to get done.

Ever wonder where the time goes? Someone has devised a method to calculate how a person would spend a typical lifespan of 70 years.

On average, a person spends 23 years sleeping, 16 years working, eight years watching TV, six years eating, six years traveling, 4.5 years of leisure time, four years treating illnesses, two years dressing, and a half year participating in religious activities.

I once read an Ann Landers column with similar calculations. A survey she quoted listed seven years in the bathroom, five years waiting in line, four years cleaning house, three years preparing meals, six months sitting at red lights and eight months opening junk mail.

I've heard it said that if you're too busy for God, you're too busy. The demands of everyday life can make it difficult to find quiet time to pray or read God's Word, not to mention telling others about Christ.

Charles Hummel, in his essay "Tyranny of the Urgent," states, "Your greatest danger is letting the urgent things crowd out the important."

C.S. Lewis penned a fable about Satan and his imps

planning their strategy to keep the world from hearing the message of salvation. One of the demons says, "I've got the plan, master. When I get on the earth and take charge of people's thinking, I'll tell them there's no heaven."

The devil responds, "Ah, they'll never believe that. The Book of Truth is full of messages about the hope of heaven through sins forgiven. They won't believe that. They know there's a glory yet future."

On the other side of the room, another says, "I've got the plan. I'll tell them there's no hell." "No good," he says. "Jesus, while He was on the earth, talked more of hell than of heaven. They know in their hearts that their wrong will have to be taken care of in some way. They deserve nothing more than hell."

And one brilliant little imp in the back stood up and said, "Then I know the answer. I'll tell them there's no hurry." And he's the one Satan chose.

We each have the same number of hours in a day; we just don't know how many years we have to spend them. The Apostle Paul reminds us to "redeem the time," meaning make the most of what we have (Ephesians 5:16 KJV). An old hymn says, "Only one life 'twill soon be passed, only what's done for Christ will last."

WE WILL NEVER FORGET!

For the past two decades on each anniversary of September 11, 2001, two words are often spoken about that horrific day when America was attacked – Never Forget!

Never forget the innocent men, women and children flying in the planes that Islamic extremists used as weapons of mass destruction to hit the Twin Towers of the World Trade Center, where thousands of workers perished.

Never forget the first responders – the policemen, fire fighters, and Port Authority personnel – who ran into the burning buildings to save as many lives as possible. Many of them died in the line of duty.

Never forget the passengers on Flight 93 who stormed the cockpit to stop the hijackers, preventing an attack likely planned for the White House or U.S. Capitol. Like the first responders, they were ordinary people who became heroes on 9/11.

Never forget individuals like Ronald Fazio who worked on the 99th floor of the World Trade Center Tower #2, who watched in horror as the first plane hit a few floors below his office. Ron started screaming for people to run to a stairwell. He went to the other side of the floor to make sure others were getting out, holding the door for them. Co-workers later learned that Ron didn't make it out.

We will never forget September 11, 2001 for the same reason we will never forget December 7, 1941 when the Japanese bombed Pearl Harbor. I learned after 9/11 that the Islamic extremists who plotted the terror attack on American soil may not have chosen a random date on the calendar.

Some historians pointed out that it's possible the

terrorists were implying that they had not forgotten the Battle of Vienna – a turning point in the Ottoman Empire's invasion of Europe. According to a BBC religion report, the Ottoman Empire, one of the largest and longest lasting empires in history, was "inspired and sustained by Islam." But they lost the Battle of Vienna, which began on September 11, 1683.

Never forget that even though evil caused suffering and tragedy, God did not leave or forsake us when those planes hit the Twin Towers and Pentagon about 9 a.m. Mark 15:25 says, "And it was the third hour, and they crucified Him" (KJV). God loved us so much that at 9 o'clock in the morning over 2000 years ago at Calvary, He was giving His only Son to die in our place for our sins.

Never forget that on that dark day in history, Jesus Christ hung on a Roman cross and for six hours experienced the most excruciating pain imaginable, so you and I can receive forgiveness and salvation.

A comforting poem by an anonymous author titled "Meet Me in the Stairwell" was emailed across the nation. Written as though a message from God, it said, "You say you will never forget where you were when you heard the news on September 11, 2001. Neither will I.... I was in the stairwell of the 23rd floor when a woman cried out to Me for help.... I was at the base of the building with the Priest ministering to the injured and devastated souls."

Knowing that the terrorists keep trying to find a way to attack us again, let us never forget to pray for America and everyone in harm's way as they protect us.

MEMORIES AND MESSAGES
ON THE REFRIGERATOR DOOR

I stared at our refrigerator door trying to decide what to do. No, I wasn't hungry, so I wasn't trying to decide what to eat.

Practically the entire door, except for the handle, was covered by memories and messages. I knew I had to do something about all that stuff. Newspaper clippings, cartoons, school photos, and drawings hugged the door, held in their places by magnets of all shapes and sizes.

Sometimes I feel the clutter around my house grows while we're sleeping or at work. At times, frustration with boxes and piles of stuff makes me determined to clean up.

I'm thinking of making it seem like fun and planning a "throwing-away party," if I can make myself part with it. However, this time it was an article in USA Weekend announcing "April 26th is Get Organized Day" that made me face the refrigerator door.

My life passed before my eyes as I sorted through the hodge-podge spread out on the kitchen table. I couldn't remember when I'd seen the refrigerator door blank. Windex and a paper towel shined the appliance.

Then came decision time. What goes and what stays? Kelley's first-grade Sunday School drawing had to stay in the upper right-hand corner of the freezer door. It's been a mainstay (though our daughter is almost 40) not just because it's a construction paper tracing of her small hand; but also because of a little yarn bow glued on her index finger and the crayon reminder, "Don't forget to pray."

Magnets on the opposite corners of the drawing had to stay – one says, "Prayer List," and the other, an inverted heart, with the message, "Thank you from the bottom of our hearts." Just under her drawing, I placed a little square magnet painted with flowers and a picket fence that reads, "Enter His gates with thanksgiving."

Beside that magnet, there's another rectangular one with Kelley's name, it's meaning, and the verse, "The Lord is my strength and my shield; my heart trusted in Him, and I am helped; therefore my heart greatly rejoiceth, and with my song will I praise Him" (Psalm 28:7 KJV). Attached to the bottom of her magnet was a round, dark blue sticker with big white letters, "Bush/Quayle '92," that would not peel off.

A larger square magnet featured a stick person drawn with a thumbprint for a body and affirming words, "You are thumbody in Him!" It fit in the upper right-hand corner of the lower door just under a magnet depicting a family of bears around a table praying, "God is grace God is good. Lettuce thank Him for our food. By this ham we are fed, give us, Lord, our raisin bread. Amen."

I just couldn't toss the Family Circle cartoon of a little girl singing, "I come from Alabama with a band-aid on my knee." Under "Prayer List," I lined up the photos of missionaries and prayer reminders from ministries like Sav-A-Life.

The pile of things I retired from the refrigerator door went into a file folder. One day, I'll organize the other side of the frig and find more memories and messages.

PRESIDENT KENNEDY AND C.S. LEWIS DIED THE SAME DAY IN 1963

I remember sitting in my third-grade classroom waiting for the bell to ring, dismissing school on November 22, 1963. When my dad walked in, I wondered why he didn't wait for me in the car. He told my teacher the President had been shot. She expressed disbelief. Then, the principal announced the tragic news over the intercom.

The same day that President John F. Kennedy was assassinated in Dallas, author and Professor C.S. Lewis died in Oxford, England. Both men's words still speak to us today. I still have *My Weekly Reader* that includes President Kennedy's inaugural speech in which he said, "And so, my fellow Americans - ask not what your country can do for you, ask what you can do for your country."

Clive Staples Lewis, born in Belfast, Ireland, studied at the University of Oxford and later taught there for over 25 years. Lewis became an atheist in his teens, but at age 33 he underwent a dramatic conversion to Christ. Biographers say his friend J.R.R. Tolkien, author of *The Lord of the Rings*, had discussions with Lewis about Christianity.

Of the more than 40 books Lewis wrote, *Mere Christianity*, published in 1952, is considered a classic. The book is a collection of radio broadcasts Lewis delivered during World War II. In it, Lewis presents an eloquent, undeniable case for believing in Christ.

"To be a Christian means to forgive the inexcusable because God has forgiven the inexcusable in you." He went on to say, "When you are arguing with Him you are arguing against the very power than makes you able to argue at all."

Lewis wrote, "At Bethlehem God became a man to

enable men to become the sons of God." He also said, "I believe in Christianity as I believe that the sun has risen: not only because I see it, but because by it I see everything else." From 1950 – 1956, C.S. Lewis penned a series of children's books called *The Chronicles of Narnia*. The seven-book series, though written for children, presents Biblical theology in an allegory form that helps children and adults understand. I think the seventh book, *The Last Battle*, is a great commentary on the book of Revelation.

Several of the best-selling books in the series have been adapted into movies - such as *The Lion, the Witch and the Wardrobe*, which tells the story of mankind's redemption from evil through the sacrificial death of the lion, Aslan, who symbolizes Christ. The books and movies remind me of one of Jesus' teaching methods. He "told them many things in parables" to help them understand His message (Matthew 13:3 NIV).

C.S. Lewis lived 64 years and John Kennedy lived 46 years. Kennedy once said, "Our most basic common link is that we all inhabit this planet. We all breathe the same air. We all cherish our children's future. And we are all mortal."

Lewis reminded Christians of the promise of eternal life in heaven, "Has this world been so kind to you that you should leave with regret? There are far, far better things ahead than any we leave behind."

LEARNING THE ABC'S OF CHRISTIAN LIFE CAN MAKE A DIFFERENCE

Years ago, while I was in college, I attended a seminar on improving memory skills. I can't remember the name of the instructor, but I do recall some of the methods he suggested when it comes to names and places.

There're all kinds of methods for storing information in your brain's memory banks. Two come to mind that most of us have used at one time or another.

First, there's an acronym, meaning a word formed from the first letter or first few letters of a series of words.

For example, radar comes from the first letters of the words "**ra**dio **d**etecting **a**nd **r**anging" and scuba from "**s**elf-**c**ontained **u**nderwater **b**reathing **a**pparatus." You'll need to know both of those acronyms if you ever play "Trivial Pursuit." To recall the five Great Lakes, use the word, HOMES for **H**uron, **O**ntario, **M**ichigan, **E**rie, **S**uperior.

Next, there's the acrostic, similar to an acronym except the letters represent a phrase or sentence. You can memorize the planets in our solar system by learning the sentence - **M**y **V**ery **E**ducated **M**other **J**ust **S**erved **U**s **N**ine **P**izzas – for **M**ercury, **V**enus, **E**arth, **M**ars, **J**upiter, **S**aturn, **U**ranus, **N**eptune, **P**luto.

Music teachers use "Every Good Boy Does Fine" to help students learn the five lines of the treble clef. "Good Boys Do Fine Always" represents the notes of the bass clef lines.

I could add several other words and phrases to this list and I'm sure you could too. I learned these when I was in grammar school and when I took piano lessons.

Though theologically speaking much could be said about the plan of salvation, the letters ABC summarize three important steps each of us must take to become a Christian.

A – Admit you are a sinner. As Romans 3:23 reminds us, "All have sinned...."

B – Believe in the Lord Jesus Christ. John 3:16 says, "Whoever believes in him should not perish, but have everlasting life."

C – Confess and leave your sin. "If we confess our sins, he is faithful and just to forgive our sins and to cleanse us from all unrighteousness" (1 John 1:9 KJV).

There's also a simple guide to help you pray based on the word, ACTS – Adoration (or praise to God), Confession, Thanksgiving, and Supplication.

As the Apostle Paul said, "....in everything by prayer and supplication, with thanksgiving, let your requests be made known unto God. And the peace of God, which surpasses all understanding, will guard your hearts and minds through Christ Jesus" (Philippians 4:6-7 NKJ).

Living the Christian life means growing "in the grace and knowledge of our Lord and Savior Jesus Christ" (2 Peter 3:18 NKJ). His grace, freely given to us though undeserved, has been defined as God's Riches At Christ's Expense. Billy Graham once said, "Becoming a Christian is a work of a moment; being a Christian is the work of a lifetime."

IN THE HEAT OF THE CRUCIBLE

Some lifelong friends of ours disciplined their young children – all three are young adults now – with a small wooden paddle. The paddle, about the size of a 12-inch ruler, had the words "Heat for the Seat" printed on it in red letters.

The parents needed only point to the paddle hanging on the wall beside the refrigerator when their children misbehaved. Reminding them of the heat they had previously felt on their seat often would immediately improve their behavior.

Heat has a way of cleaning and purifying. Metals and ores are purified when melted with intense heat in a container sometimes called a crucible.

I once heard a minister describe a crucible and how a refiner went about his work of purifying the metal. He described a large, tall vessel like a vat. The refiner would watch the boiling caldron from a seat perched on the side of the crucible.

Any impurities in a precious metal such as gold would rise to the surface of the molten mixture. The refiner would use a tool to skim the dross off the hot, liquid metal until all the impurities were removed.

The minister concluded his sermon illustration relating how the refiner knew the metal was purified – when he could see his unblemished reflection on the surface.

Although we are created in the image of God (Genesis 1:26), the impurity of our sin mars His reflection in us. It takes the fiery trials of life to purify us. The Apostle Peter tells us, "Think it not strange concerning the fiery trial which is to try you" (1 Peter 4:12 KJV).

A crucible can also be defined as a severe test or trial. Though I wish I could say it isn't so, trials and tests show me what I'm really made of. My crucible may be for my correction or just a trial of my faith. But I find consolation in the fact that I learn to be more Christ-like from being in the crucible.

Peter also writes, "That the trial of your faith, being more precious than gold that perishes, though it be tried with fire, might be found unto praise and honor and glory" at Christ's appearing" (1 Peter 1:7 KJV).

As one author has said, "A clay pot in the sun will always be a clay pot. It has to go through the white heat of the furnace to become porcelain."

Charles Spurgeon has written, "The good that I have received from my sorrows and pains and griefs, is altogether incalculable. What do I not owe to the hammer and the anvil, the fire and the file? What do I not owe to the crucible and the furnace, the bellows that have blown up the coals and the hand which has thrust me into the heat?"

Remember the words of Spurgeon while going through fiery trials, "As sure as God puts his children in the furnace, He will be in the furnace with them."

RECIPE FOR THANKSGIVING: GRACE AND GRATITUDE

Thanksgiving season brings back memories of two pictures I've seen in many homes through the years. Often, the pair are hung side by side on the wall near a kitchen or dining room table.

The pictures look like portraits of an elderly couple. A white-haired old man with a beard, his hands clasped and pressed against his forehead, seems to be praying. Beside him on the table where he is seated one can see a small loaf of bread, knife, bowl and a Family Bible with eye glasses folded and lying on top of it. His picture is titled "Grace."

A second picture shows a wrinkled woman with silver white, wavy hair seated at a table, an open Bible in front of her with eye glasses resting on a page of Scripture. She, too, has her hands clasped as though in prayer. Next to the Bible, there's a small loaf of bread and a wedge of cheese on a wooden plate near a cream-colored ceramic pitcher. Her picture is called "Gratitude."

The two actually never met each other. The picture of the old gentleman dates back to World War I. In 1918, a peddler named Charles Wilden, who sold boot scrapers, knocked on the door of photographer Eric Enstrom in Bovey, Minnesota. According to historical accounts of their chance meeting, Enstrom was preparing a portfolio of pictures to take to the Minnesota Photographers Association convention.

Enstrom reportedly commented, "I wanted to take a picture that would show people that even though they had to do without many things because of the war, they still had much to be thankful for." He saw something in the kind face of the peddler and asked him to pose for a picture at the table as though he were praying over a meager meal. A businessman wrote about the picture in a newspaper column, and "Grace" became an iconic symbol of thanksgiving.

With the popularity of "Grace," an Indiana gift company named Dickson began searching for a companion portrait of an elderly woman during the 1960's. Over 1000 photos were submitted, but not one of them was selected. When Jack Garren, owner of a religious bookstore in Centralia, Illinois, found out about the search, he immediately suggested his grandmother, Mrs. Myrtle Copple.

For years, people had commented how the old man in "Grace" resembled Myrtle's father. Garren convinced his grandmother to pose for a series of photographs, seated at a table with an open Bible, her head bowed and hands folded. "Gratitude" became as popular as "Grace," with thousands of pictures sold.

When you gather around the table with your family this Thanksgiving, remember to say grace and offer gratitude to God for all He provides. Jesus gave us an example to follow when He took "the five loaves and the two fish, and looking up to heaven, he blessed and broke and gave the loaves to the disciples, and the disciples gave them to the multitude" (Matthew 14:19 NKJ).

"Gratitude grows from a seed called grace," writes Louie Giglio. Live each day with an attitude of gratitude and grow in grace.

QUADRIPELGIC ANSWERS QUESTION OF WHY PEOPLE SUFFER

Joni Erickson Tada celebrated her 70th birthday in 2019. That birthday marked a milestone, but not just because of her age. Joni has lived 52 of those 70 years confined to a wheelchair.

In 1967, Joni dove into shallow water in the Chesapeake Bay. In seconds, her life changed from athletic teenager to quadriplegic. She was paralyzed from her shoulders down, due to a broken neck. Back then, Joni says, doctors thought it impossible for a quadriplegic to reach age 70.

But in spite of her tragic circumstances, she has overcome bitterness, endured suffering, and still found meaning in life. In 1976, Joni wrote about her life-changing experience in an autobiography that was retold in a movie called "Joni," released in 1980. She became a talented artist, painting beautiful drawings by holding a small paintbrush in her mouth.

Joni Erickson Tada now lives in California and leads a ministry for people with disabilities and their families. Through her ministry, Joni & Friends, some 10,000 wheelchairs are collected every year and distributed in over 86 countries. Week-long Family Retreats are held for those who live with disability.

She released a video on her 70th birthday that I have watched numerous times. Her words eloquently answer the question of why people suffer. And, since I enjoy photography, I could literally picture her explanation and wanted to share her words with you.

"I am living well. I'm living joyfully. Yes, a broken neck is a tragedy, but God has the capacity, get this, to look at our suffering through a narrow lens and a wide angle one. When God looks at a painful event through a narrow lens, like my broken neck, He sees the tragedy for what it is and He is deeply grieved…God felt the sting in his chest when I dove into shallow water and crunched my neck and severed my spinal cord.

"But when God looked at it through his wide-angle lens, He saw the tragedy in relation to everything leading up to it, as well as flowing out of it. He saw Joni and Friends…. He saw Family Retreats and He saw 'Wheels for the World'…. He saw hundreds of thousands of people with disabilities, and their families, coming to Jesus Christ.

"He saw this amazing mosaic stretching into eternity. And friend, it's this mosaic with all its parts, both good and evil, which brings God utter delight. And so, as I turn 70, I'm saying NO to a narrow view of my life…I'm not gonna go down that dark grim path. And I encourage you to do the same."

Joni asks us to say, "Jesus, give me faith to believe in your wide-angle view of the difficult things that happen in my life. Give me your perspective so I can delight in the beautiful mosaic that one day I'm gonna understand."

Joni's message reminded me of the description of Jesus, who understands "the feeling of our infirmities" (Hebrews 4:15). She once said, "There's no inherent goodness in my spinal cord injury; it is an awful thing, but a wonderful, miracle-making God can take something awful in a life and pronounce it good through the application of His grace."

Joni, you inspire my faith in God!

THE WAY TO GOD
IS FOUND IN THE MANGER

Every year when it's time to decorate our home at Christmas, I sort through the boxes of decorations and ornaments for the tree.

One box of decorations holds a collection of angels made of wood and ceramics that we place on our mantle and bookshelves. Tucked away in a box I most look forward to opening is a small wooden stable and set of miniature people and animals.

The manger scene, sometimes called a crèche, re-enacts the Christmas story. I've seen crèches that would fit in a shoebox and others, usually outdoors, that are almost life-size. No matter what their size, the figurines of Mary and Joseph and other characters are turned toward the Christ-child lying in the manger.

Ever wonder who came up with the idea for the first crèche? Historians credit St. Francis of Assisi (1182-1226 A.D.) whose first crèche, or Christmas Crib, was a simple manger with a doll in it. Children brought gifts there and older adults came with their prayers. Later, animals borrowed from neighbors were added to the scene.

Whenever I look at a crèche, I'm reminded of one of my favorite Christmas carols – "Away in a Manger." The words come from a poem found in a Lutheran Sunday School book published in 1885 in Philadelphia.

The first two verses of "Away in a Manger" appeared anonymously in *Little Children's Book for Schools and Families*. Verse three was written in the early 1900's by a Methodist minister named John Thomas McFarland for a church children's program.

A manger is really the last place you'd expect to find a baby. It's a feed-box! The manger has been described as a "testament in wood and straw." It was where the shepherds came to worship the newborn King.

Sometimes, when I sing "Away in a Manger," I wonder if there shouldn't be another verse or at least another title for the song. Maybe it should be called "The Way in a Manger."

Jesus said, "I am the way, the truth and the life. No one comes to the Father, except through me" (John 14:6 NIV). The only way to God is through His Son, Jesus Christ.

A story is told of a missionary traveling to a remote village to train leaders of the local church. A guide was selected to take him to the village because the only way to reach this remote place was to walk through the jungle.

The journey started out without much of a problem; the path was easy to follow. Soon, however, the path literally disappeared as the guide cut a way through the jungle undergrowth with his machete.

The missionary grew concerned and asked, "Where is the path?" The guide smiled; looking back he told the missionary, "I am the path." So, it is with Christ – He is our path to God. When you see a crèche this Christmas season may it remind you of "The Way" in a manger.

THE GIFT EXCHANGE
THAT WILL CHANGE YOUR LIFE

"Christmas wouldn't be Christmas without presents," author Louisa Mae Alcott's character, Jo, says in her book, *Little Women*.

But it's not always easy to know what presents to give the special people on our Christmas list. That's the reason someone has said, "More Christmas gifts are exchanged after Christmas than on Christmas Day."

Why? It could be the person doesn't want that gift because it's not the color they would've chosen. Then again, it could be the wrong size. Stores brace for this after-Christmas rush to return gifts.

There's one perfect gift I wish everyone could receive, not just at Christmas, but also every day of the year. Just like the gifts we give each other, you must accept this gift with open arms to receive it. Best of all, it's a gift you can never outgrow. It's perfect for all ages.

When you receive this gift, it also comes with an exchange. You exchange your old life for a new life, and this is not just any life. "The gift of God is eternal life through Jesus Christ our Lord" (Romans 6:23).

This gift will change how you live your life. The Old Testament prophet Isaiah said Jesus would exchange beauty for ashes, the oil of joy for mourning, and the garment of praise for the spirit of despair (Isaiah 61:3).

People who walk in darkness exchange their darkness for the Light of the World. Once they were blind, but now they can see.

You and I can't buy this gift. None of us deserve it, but it's free to all those who believe and receive. What could a man, woman, or child give in exchange for his soul anyway? (Matthew 16:26) For by grace (we are) saved through faith, and that not of ourselves; it is the gift of God (Ephesians 2:8 KJV). This gift is not just for the present, you also are given a "future and a hope" (Jeremiah 29:11 NKJ).

Someone once said, "Who you are is God's gift to you, who you become is your gift to God." You and I have been given the gift of life, there's no greater gift that we can give than to present ourselves to God.

The greatest gift mankind was ever given came wrapped in swaddling clothes. Then, thirty-three years later, He was hung on a tree to die for you and me. His followers wrapped his body in grave clothes. Now we can be clothed in newness of life.

Christmas wouldn't be Christmas without Christ! Unwrap the love, peace, and joy that came from a tiny little boy born in a humble stable in Bethlehem. A 3rd century theologian once wrote that Christ "became human that we might become divine; he revealed himself in a body that we might understand the unseen Father."

"Thanks be to God for His indescribable gift" (2 Corinthians 9:15 NKJ).

WHAT IF WE SHARED SEASON'S GREETINGS YEAR-ROUND?

"Merry Christmas!" I've been saying this seasonal greeting everywhere I go, along with "Happy New Year!"

I'm on a mission to greet as many people as possible for Charlie because he's not here to do it. He left us in December 1997, so he has spent a number of Christmases with Christ, whom he loved and served.

If you ever met Charlie Smith, you heard him say, "Merry Christmas and Happy New Year," not just in December, but year-round. For those of you who never knew him, let me introduce you.

Charlie worked as an accountant for 24 years until he began losing his eyesight, a painfully slow process that continued for decades, resulting in blindness. His failing eyesight forced him to retire at age 45.

But Charlie didn't complain about his circumstances, even when an unexplainable bright light flashed on and off in his eyes every moment of his life for the last few years. Every Wednesday for more than 16 years, he conducted a weekly service at a local nursing home.

He would also visit the residents who couldn't come to the lobby for the service, going room to room letting them know someone cared. When asked what a person who gives so much of himself for so long receives in return, Charlie said, "I've been paid back many times over in my life. You may go in the door feeling blah, but always feel good when you leave."

Then he went on to talk about how the residents were a joy to be around, even though he had seen them at times when they were lonely, sick or depressed. His genuine caring flowed from his faith in God, whom he believed deserved all the glory for any good works.

What better principles to live by each day than cheerfully giving to others as God did when He gave us His greatest gift, Jesus Christ. What if we thought about others before ourselves?

Think of what the world would be like if we lived each day as though it was the first day of a new year. Wouldn't we have a more joyful outlook on life if we put the past behind us and looked forward to each new day?

If we actually lived "Merry Christmas" and "Happy New Year" year-round, we would be human messengers bringing "glory to God in the highest, and on earth peace, goodwill toward men" (Luke 2:14 KJV).

What was Charlie communicating? "Merry" means cheerful, and "Christmas" is a celebration of Jesus' birth, as well as a time for giving and thinking of others. "Happy" is defined as joy and contentment. A "new year" speaks of a fresh start or clean slate of time.

By his 72 years of life, Charlie Smith demonstrated what it means to be a Christian because he was a reflection of Christ. He could see those around him through eyes of compassion. Live every day with "Merry Christmas and "Happy New Year" in your heart, and share it with others!

MAKE THE CROSS
YOUR TURNING POINT

While driving through the Conecuh National Forest in the southern corner of Covington County, AL, you'll find the Blue Lake United Methodist Camp.

It's a beautiful place where church camps and other meetings are held throughout the year. I like to call it "holy ground" because of the blessings I've received when I attended events there.

If you've ever visited Blue Lake, you've seen something that makes this body of water unique. A pair of crosses, planted in the shoreline, face each other on opposite sides of the lake.

During the day, the 20-foot-tall crosses cast a shadow across the mirror-like surface of the water. At night, the crosses with their neon/fluorescent lights illuminate the darkness between the tall trees in the forest surrounding Blue Lake.

Evidently, the glow from the crosses is visible in the skies above Blue Lake. Several years ago, electrical service was interrupted by a storm – leaving the crosses unlit for a period of time. While attending an Air Show at what is now called the South Alabama Regional Airport, the camp director met a helicopter pilot who asked about the status of the crosses.

The gentleman explained that the crosses signaled the turning around point for their pilots. The light from the crosses in the midst of the towering pines gave the aviators crucial direction for their flight pattern. It was their turning around point to head back to the base.

A week or so later, the person called, asking about the

cost to repair the crosses. Then, he mailed a check to cover the amount. The crosses shined in the darkness once again.

Far from Blue Lake on a hill called Calvary, there stood a cross made of wooden beams where Jesus was crucified over 2,000 years ago. His cross remains a beacon of hope to a lost and dying world searching for truth.

It's where people like you and me find our turning around point. At the cross, we turn from sin and going our own way and begin following Jesus Christ who is "the way, the truth, and the life" (John 14:6 KJV). A seventh century church leader has written, "How splendid the cross of Christ! It brings life, not death; light, not darkness; paradise, not its loss."

Like a shining light in a dark place, the cross gives us crucial direction for our lives. This turning point changes our destination from eternal destruction to eternal life. Jesus, "the light of the world," died so we could find forgiveness for our sins. His death paid the cost for our sins.

Have you been to the cross? A.W. Tozer once said, "The cross of Christ is the most revolutionary thing ever to appear among men." A hymn writer expressed it this way, "There's room at the cross for you. Though millions have come, there's still room for one. there's room at the cross for you."

Come to the cross of Christ. Ask Jesus to forgive your sins. Have you lost your way? Come back to the cross of Christ. Today could be your "turning point."

THE OLD RUGGED CROSS OF CHRIST CHANGED HISTORY, CHANGES LIVES

There's a story told of a British soldier during World War I who fled the battlefield and deserted his regiment one night. He headed for the coast to find a boat to England and ended up hopelessly lost, wandering around in the dark night.

The soldier came across what he thought was a signpost and began to climb it. If he could read it, he might find out which direction to go. As he reached the top of the pole, he struck a match. The flicker of light revealed an unexpected sight.

He found himself looking into the face of Jesus Christ. Instead of a signpost, he had climbed up a roadside crucifix. Clinging to that cross, the soldier remembered that Christ had died for him. Christ had endured suffering and never turned back. The next morning the soldier returned to the trenches.

Oswald Chambers writes, "The Cross did not happen to Jesus: He came on purpose for it." Chambers adds, "The whole meaning of the Incarnation is the Cross. The Cross is the center of time and of eternity."

Christ changed the history of the world. History is His story. Everything in history is measured as B.C. (before Christ) or A.D. (Anno Domini – Latin for "in the year of our Lord") since His birth. Someone once said, "You do not understand Christ, unless you understand the Cross." Author John Bisagno states, "Christianity is a cross, and cross is 'I' crossed out."

Theologian Andrew Murray has said, "As you gaze upon the cross, and long for conformity to him, be not weary or fearful because you cannot express in words what you seek. Ask him to plant the cross in your heart. Believe in him, the crucified and now living one, to dwell within you, and breathe his own mind there."

The Apostle Paul put it this way, "I am crucified with Christ: nevertheless I live; yet not I, but Christ liveth in me: and the life which I now live in the flesh I live by the faith of the Son of God, who loved me, and gave himself for me" (Galatians 2:20 KJV).

A.W. Tozer explains, "To be crucified means three things. First, the man who is crucified is facing only one direction. If he hears anything behind him, he can't turn around to see what's going on. He has stopped looking back. The crucified man on the cross is looking in only one direction and that is the direction of God and Christ and the Holy Spirit."

While going through some personal spiritual troubles, George Bennard began to reflect on the meaning of the Cross and penned the words, "On a hill far away stood an old rugged cross, the emblem of suffering and shame; and I love that old cross where the dearest and best for a world of lost sinners was slain."

"The Cross of Christ is the heart of the Gospel," according to evangelist Reinhard Bonnke. G. Campbell Morgan has written, "Nobody who has truly seen the Cross of Christ can ever again speak of hopeless cases." As another hymn writer put it, "Kneel at the Cross, Christ will meet you there."

GOD, NOT THE DEVIL, IS IN THE DETAILS

Several weeks ago, while listening to Faith Radio (WLBF Montgomery, AL), I heard a minister named Charles Swindoll teaching about Jesus raising Lazarus from the dead.

During his message, he quoted the words of Edward MacCartney, "Sometimes we can learn more from the silence of the dead than the speech of the living." Swindoll said the quote came from MacCartney's book, *Bible Epitaphs*.

I decided to find out more about MacCartney and his writings. Reverend Clarence Edward MacCartney was the pastor of the First Presbyterian Church in Pittsburg, Pennsylvania from 1927 - 1957. He also pastored in Philadelphia and authored dozens of books.

Bible Epitaphs, published in 1936, studies the lives of 17 Bible characters from which he wrote biographical sermons. My curiosity, as well as my love of books, sent me to an online retailer selling copies of old books hard to find or no longer in print. I chose one vendor from the list. Then I clicked on the Thrift Store and ordered a copy said to be in "good condition," including the book jacket.

About two weeks later, a small package arrived in the mail. Turns out the Thrift Store is located in St. Louis, Missouri. I opened the package, anxious to see what I'd purchased. To my delightful surprise and excitement, I read the handwritten signature of the original owner of the book.

J. Calvin Holsinger, History Dept., State College, Bloomsburg, Penn. I could not believe my eyes. Dr. Holsinger was my History Professor at Evangel College in Springfield, Missouri, 40 years ago. I recalled a Facebook post that I read last year with the news that the 89-year-old retired professor had died.

Then, I looked up his obituary and found that he had taught at Pennsylvania State College early in his education career.

The odds of this happening to me cannot be calculated. The experience defies explanation. It seemed God winked at me. Author Squire Rushnell, in his book *When God Winks at You*, writes, "Every time you receive what some call a coincidence or an answered prayer, it's a direct and personal message of reassurance from God to you--what I call a godwink.

"In this book I aim to show that every godwink that happens in your life is a very personal experience," Rushnell observes as he introduces in his book stories about people who experienced a godwink. "Like those stories. The instant you receive a godwink, you'll know it."

Another one of my favorite authors, Elizabeth Elliot, once wrote, "If you believe in a God who controls the big things, you have to believe in a God who controls the little things." I've heard it said, "The devil is in the details," regarding items hidden in the fine print. But in the words attributed to Michelangelo, "God is in the details."

God is an expert in details. After all, He numbers "the very hairs of your head" (Luke 12:7 KJV). He brought all these circumstances together at the exact time for me. I knew without a doubt it was a personal message from God.

FAITH OVER FEAR
IN THE FACE OF COVID-19

Since the COVID-19 pandemic began in early 2020, I have watched the news reports and read news articles about the symptoms and how to prevent the spread of this Coronavirus.

At first, our local numbers remained low. It seemed that COVID-19 was occurring primarily in metropolitan areas with large populations. As the number of people testing positive increased in rural south Alabama, I realized COVID-19 was spreading close to home.

Then the lockdown was announced and schools, churches, business, and government…basically, our way of life, came to a halt as people isolated in their home for several weeks of quarantine. Life took on a new normal with people wearing masks, washing their hands often during the day, and standing six feet apart. I tried to practice these precautions, which gave me a sense of security even though I knew COVID-19 was highly contagious.

In August 2020, someone in our family was exposed to COVID-19. There's really no way to know the source. Within a week, my husband, our daughter, our son-in-law, my mother-in-law, my aunt and I all tested positive. We followed our doctor's instructions and took the medicines prescribed. Thankfully, our family members all recovered.

Hearing the words, "you tested positive," struck fear in my heart, as well as each time we learned another family member tested positive. Fever, chills, diarrhea and nausea, body aches, intense fatigue, loss of appetite and other symptoms afflicted our bodies. This column would be the length of a short story if I tried to explain the details we learned about this dangerous disease.

Now that our family members have survived COVID-19, I can truly say that God's Word, prayer, and worship music helped me overcome fear with faith. We witnessed the many ways God was walking with us through the valley of the shadow of COVID-19. God has used this sickness to rekindle my faith. That's what happens when you have to depend completely on God.

Best-selling author Max Lucado told *The Christian Post*, "We've never lived in a time like this. This is unprecedented…. Yet the Bible tells us that times have been bizarre before. You open your Bible and…read about pestilence, fears, dark times. The Bible is written for times like this."

Lucado went on to say, "I think this is a time where we need to be feeding our faith. If you feed your faith, your fears will starve. If you feed your fears, your faith will starve. Our tendency is to feed our fears. We have to do intentional things to feed our faith."

Reading scriptures fed my faith. "Fear not, for I am with you. Be not dismayed for I am your God. I will strengthen you, Yes, I will help you," (Isaiah 41:10 NKJ). "For God has not given us a spirit of fear, but of power and of love and of a sound mind" (2 Timothy 1:7 NKJ). God's promises do not change. He will never leave us or forsake us.

Bible teacher Tony Evans put it this way, "As we face the COVID-19 crisis together, we should trade our fears for trust as we are going through this trial. Now is the time to draw near to God and to draw near to one another." I am thankful for friends who prayed for our family!

DISCOVER BEST ADVICE BOOK FOR THE NEW YEAR

The wit and wisdom of Benjamin Franklin made his *Poor Richard's Almanac* popular. He published it every year from 1733-1758.

Almanacs traditionally include a calendar, facts about outstanding dates and events, and weather predictions especially useful for knowing when to plant crops.

Another thing that almanacs are known for is practical advice. Ben Franklin's gave us classic sayings like, "Early to bed, early to rise, makes a man healthy, wealthy and wise" and "Work as if you were to live a hundred years, pray as if you were to die tomorrow."

Franklin made several wise statements about time. In 1746, he wrote in his almanac, "Lost time is never found again." We still repeat his advice to a young tradesman, "Remember that time is money."

He also penned these profound words, "Dost thou love life? Then do not squander time; for that's the stuff life is made of."

Others have written about the subject. Philosopher William James once stated, "The great use of life is to spend it for something that will outlast it." Or as another writer has said, "Counting time is not nearly so important as making time count."

Thomas Edison remarked, "Time is not a commodity that can be stored for the future. It must be invested hour by hour, or else it is gone forever." Helen Keller said, "I will not just live my life. I will not just spend my life. I will invest my life."

Though books abound on how to live your life, the

wisest advice can be found in the best book ever written –
the Bible. The inspired Word of God gives us words of
wisdom to live by. Every day is a gift from God according
to Psalm 118:24, "This is the day the Lord has made; we will
rejoice and be glad in it" (NKJ).

Ephesians 5:16 tells us we are living in evil times, so
make every day count. Jesus even said that in this life we
would have trouble, but to be of good cheer for He had
overcome the world; so, we can overcome too. Those who
wait upon the Lord shall renew their strength (John 16:33,
Isaiah 40:31).

Life is uncertain. Solomon, the wisest mortal who ever
lived, observed that we do not know what a day may bring
forth (Proverbs 27:1). Anyone who watches the evening
news certainly understands the truth of his words.

Trust God even when life doesn't make sense. "Trust in
the Lord with all your heart and lean not on your own
understanding. In all your ways acknowledge Him and He
shall direct your path," Solomon instructs us (Proverbs 3,
verses 5 and 6 NKJ).

Don't worry or be anxious about tomorrow nor today.
Jesus said there's more to life than what to eat and what to
wear. "Seek first the kingdom of God, and his righteousness
and all these things shall be added to you" (Matthew 6:33
NKJ).

During the coming year, search the Scriptures for
wisdom to live each day.

ACKNOWLEDGEMENTS

I want to thank my husband, Greg, for helping make this book a reality. He has always been my editor and proofreader. Because of Greg's encouragement and persistence, you are reading *Everyday Faith for Daily Life*.

Thank you to everyone involved in this book project: Walt Merrell, who wrote the foreword; Scott Dawson, Mark Rhoades, and Brenda Gantt, who wrote endorsements; and Cheryl Cotton for her expertise on the cover design. Special thanks to Paul and Linda Linzey with P&L Publishing for their knowledge and guidance through the publication process.

And, I want to thank all the readers of my weekly religion column through the years. Your positive feedback let me know my words were speaking to hearts and lives.

ABOUT THE AUTHOR

Jan White has written a weekly religion column for over 25 years in the *Andalusia Star-News* and the *Enterprise Southeast Sun,* as well as other newspapers. She is an award-winning writer. Among her numerous writing awards, Jan received the prestigious Amy Writing Award for one of her columns selected from submissions of writers nationwide. Her articles and devotionals have been published in *Focus on the Family* and *Charisma Magazine,* as well as other publications.

She has worked for three newspapers, and written articles for two ministries. Jan graduated from Evangel University in Springfield, MO, with a B.S. in History and English/Journalism. Jan and her husband, Greg, live in Andalusia, Alabama, where she is active as a community volunteer, and loves being Grandma Jan to two granddaughters.

Contact Information

Website: www.janwhitewriter.com
Facebook:https://www.facebook.com/jan.white.9237

Made in the USA
Columbia, SC
20 December 2020